My name is Bob

Cute Dogs

Craft Your Own Pooches

By Chie Hayano

for lovers of little dogs

Itsy-Bitsy Pooches
Bob's Story

Preface

"Miniature stuffed animals."

That's what I came to call them as I continued to make itsy-bitsy little critters. Little friends that fit in the palm of your hand. People often ask me why I don't make bigger ones, but to me, their smallness is what makes them so fun. When I think about it, all my favorite stories that I read when I was a child always featured a tiny little character, hiding in the main character's pocket or in the corner of a room. That kind of magical and mysterious, exciting feeling is what I get when I make these mini stuffed animals. I always liked to painstakingly craft little things, but the reason I started making miniature stuffed animals was that I found a little teddy bear about 2 1/2 inches tall at a store while on a trip about four years ago. Until then, I hadn't really thought, "I love teddy bears!" But I was fascinated with its construction; the arms and legs moved even though it was so tiny! I was stunned by the fact that it had paw pads on its feet—even claws!

After that, I decided to make tiny teddy bears myself. As I tried making similar bears, I began to feel that I'd like to make all kinds of stuffed animals, not just bears.

Then one day I saw a stuffed dog that someone had made. It was amazing—too lifelike and with too much presence to just call it a stuffed animal. I remember being really surprised and moved by it. I've never seen such a handcrafted dog before. My wish is to make those kinds of lifelike miniature stuffed animals. That's the feeling that I had when I made the miniature cute dogs that you'll encounter in this book. I would like those of you who love making little things to have fun crafting these itsy-bitsy teeny-tiny pooches as a watchdog for your desk, or as a miniature version of the dog that you actually own, or for a friend who can't own a real dog. The possibilities are endless—Yes! Make him a little doghouse, or puppy clothes! Or how about little toys for your miniature stuffed animal? I hope you have fun continuing to expand the little world you create.

Contents

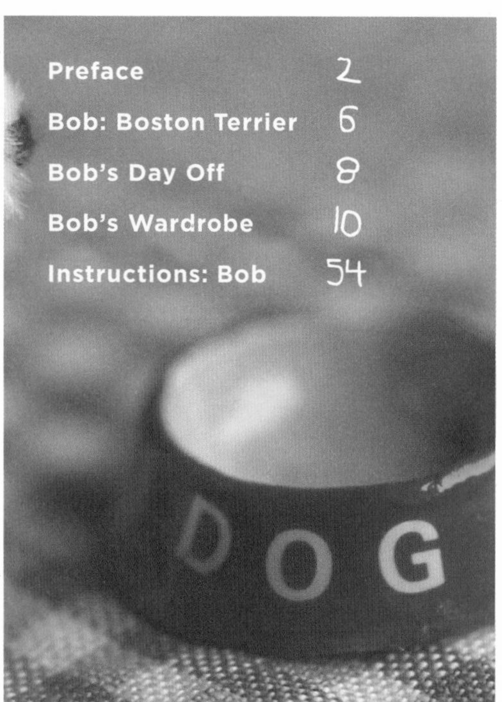

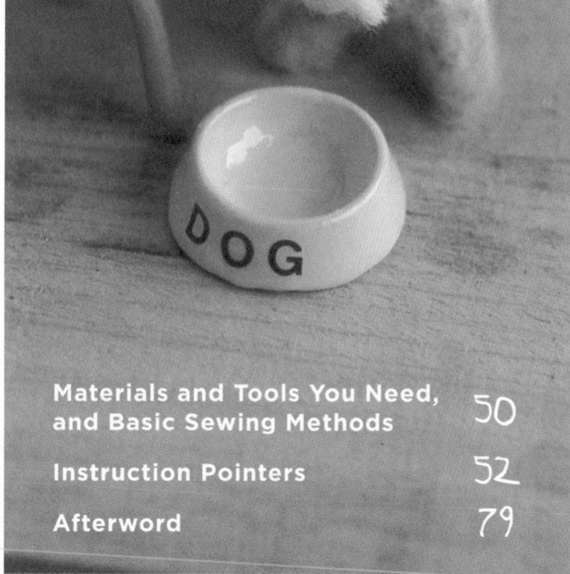

My name is

Bob

Bob: Boston Terrier

I'm charming.
I'm good at upward glances.

Instructions p. 54

Bob: Boston Terrier
I'm charming.

Bob's Day Off

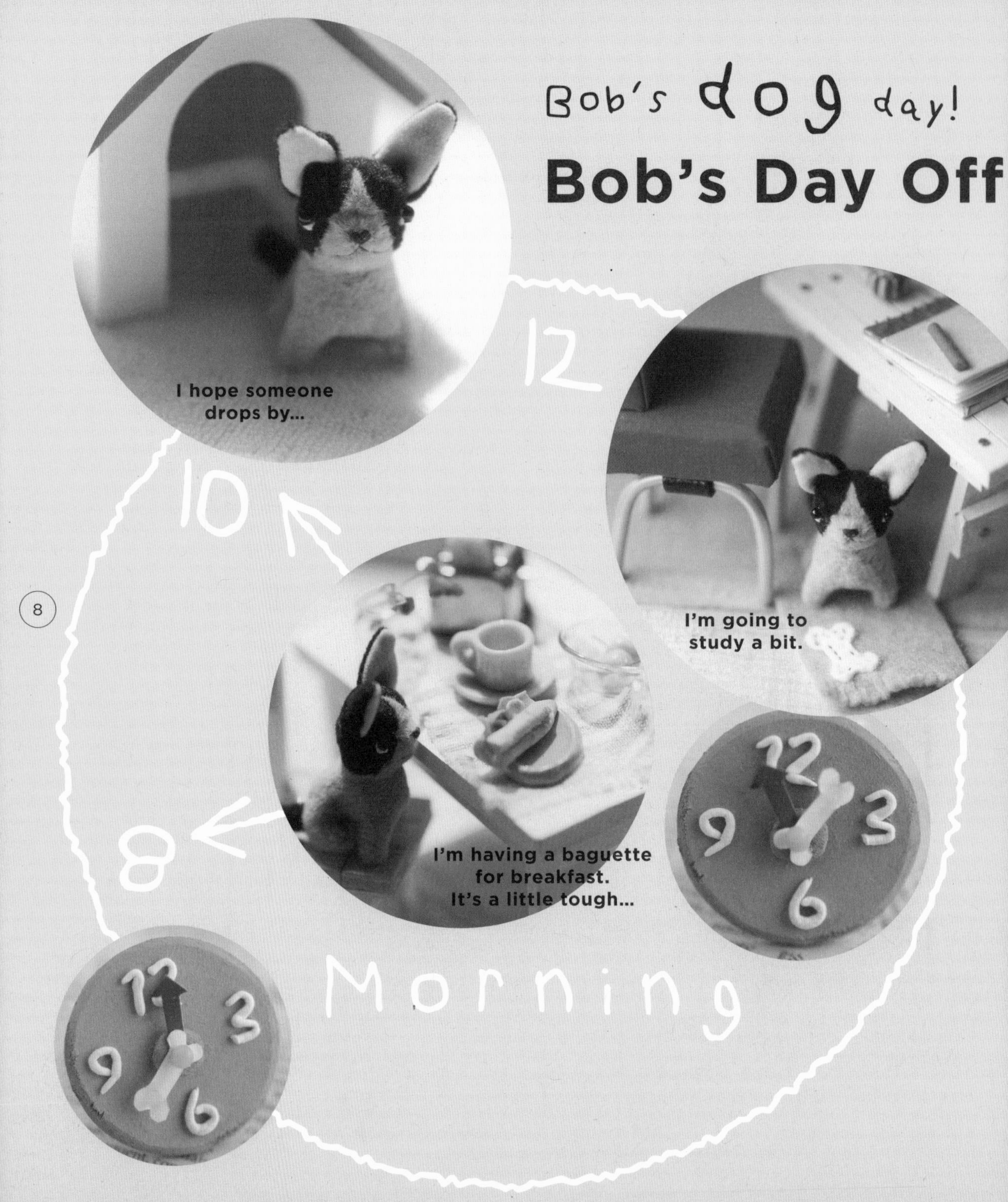

Bob's dog day!
I hope someone drops by...
12
10
I'm going to study a bit.
I'm having a baguette for breakfast. It's a little tough...
8
12
9
3
6
12
3
9
6
Morning

12
9
3
6

2

Afternoon

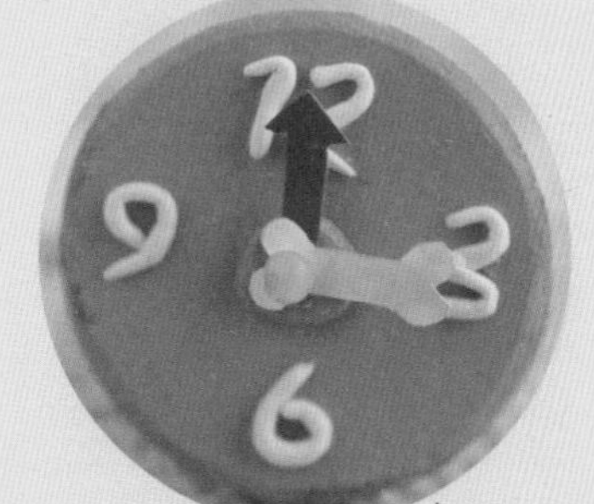
12
9
3
6

3

It feels nice to take a walk.

6

I ran into Robin. We're having a snack together.

I like playing dress-up...

Someone gave me a reindeer costume last year as a Christmas present. I'd have preferred a piece of beef jerky, but anyway...

Bob's Wardrobe

The baby chick pattern is my favorite. How do I look?

Bob's Wardrobe

*

a.b.c.....

11

I sometimes transform into superman, too. Why am I the only one always dressing up?

Lulu: Chihuahua

I'm timid.
It's not that I get scared easily,
I'm just careful, you know.

Instructions p. 54

Lulu: Chihuahua
I'm timid.

My name is

Chibi

Chibi:
pomeranian
I'm shy.

Chibi: Pomeranian

I'm shy.
But what I really want is to be friends!

Instructions p. 61

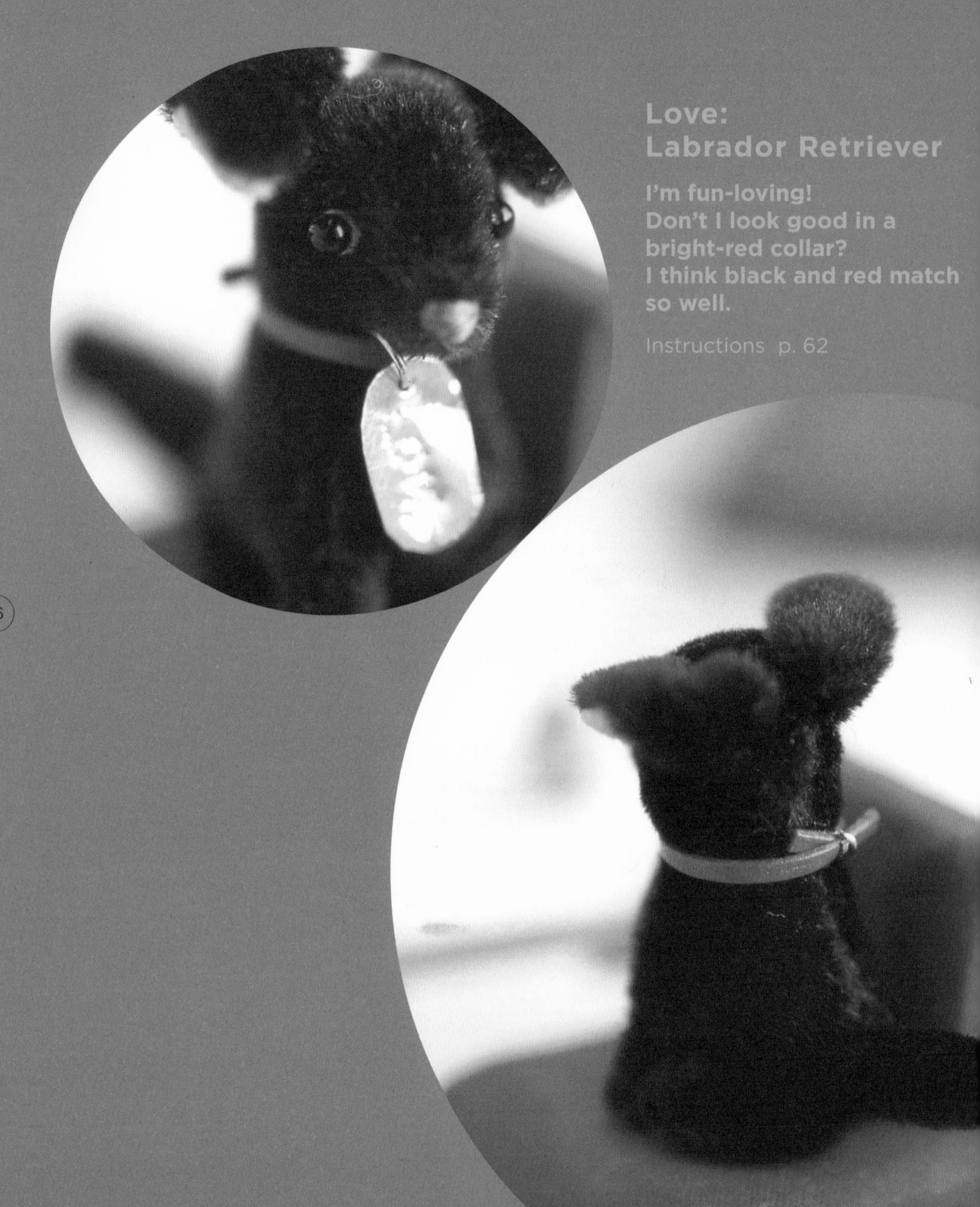

Love: Labrador Retriever

I'm fun-loving! Don't I look good in a bright-red collar? I think black and red match so well.

Instructions p. 62

Love:

Labrador Retriever
I'm fun-loving!

My name is
Love

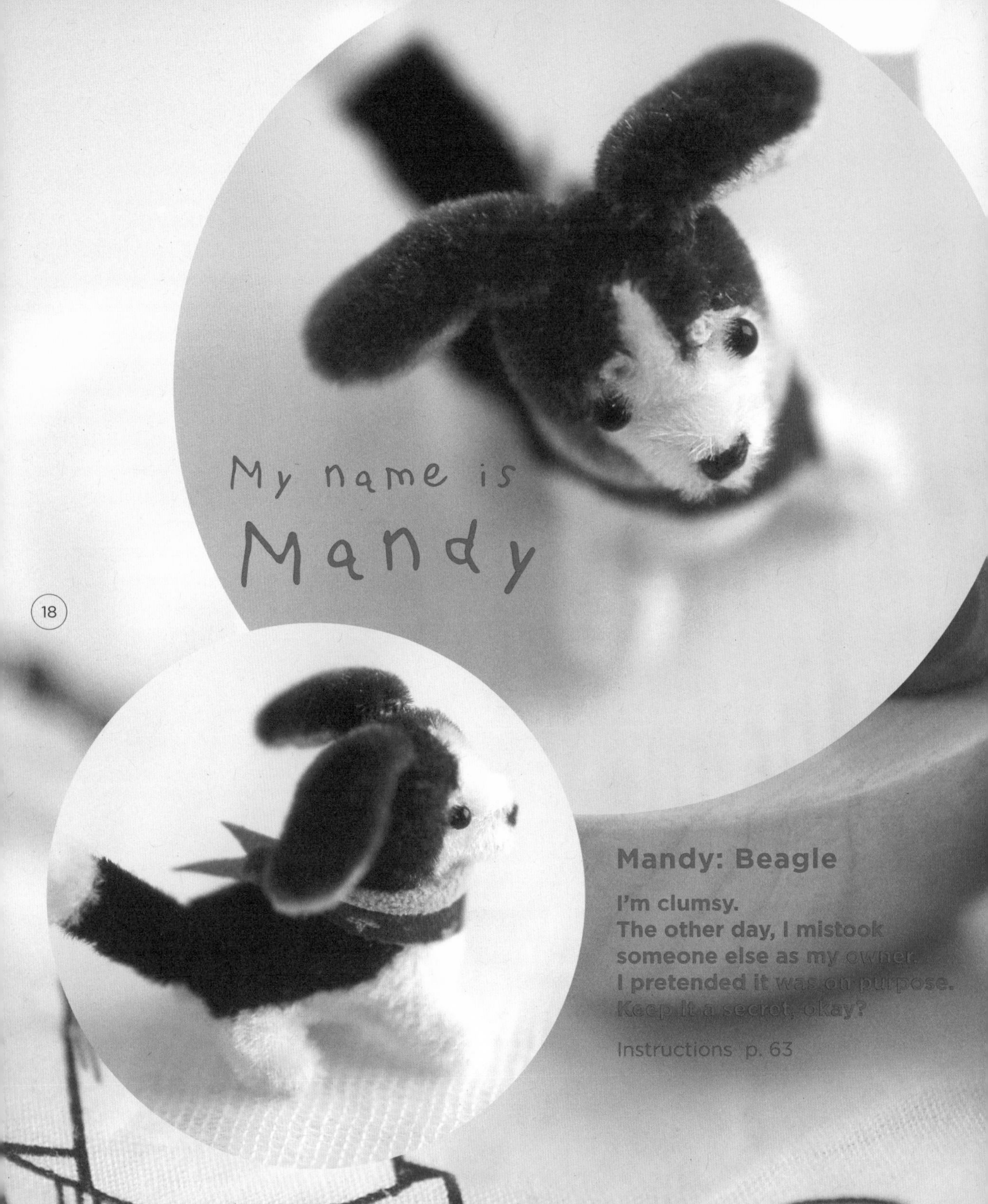

My name is Mandy

Mandy: Beagle

I'm clumsy.
The other day, I mistook someone else as my owner.
I pretended it was on purpose.
Keep it a secret, okay?

Instructions p. 63

Mandy:

Beagle
I'm clumsy.

Bingo.

Bull Terrier
I'm always
hungry!

Bingo: Bull Terrier

I'm always hungry.
If someone tells me,
"I'm going go give you a treat,"
I follow him.
I mean, who can resist
something yummy?

Instructions p. 64

My name is Bingo

Wendy

White Terrier
I like to be
around people.

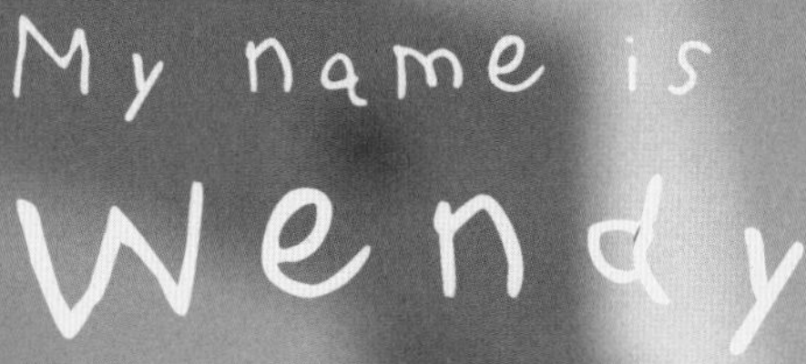
My name is
Wendy

Wendy: White Terrier

**I like to be around people.
I don't like being left alone.
Let's hang out!**

Instructions p. 65

My name is

Champ

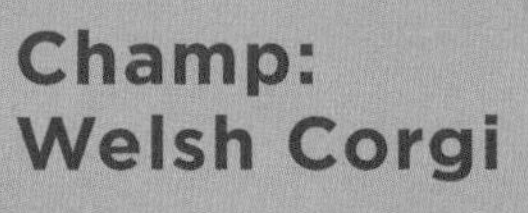

Champ: Welsh Corgi

**I'm mischievous.
I hide my owner's favorite pair of sneakers when he isn't around.
Heehee...**

Instructions p. 66

Champ:

Welsh Corgi
I'm mischievous.

RADIO FLYER

Coke: Miniature Dachshund

I'm smart.
What's on top of a house? Roof!
What's sandpaper feel like? Rough!
Ruff!
I'm so smart.

Instructions p. 67

We are Pepsi & Coke

Pepsi: Miniature Dachshund

I'm full of curiosity.
I want so see this and t
I want to see everythin
I'm so excited.

Instructions p. 67

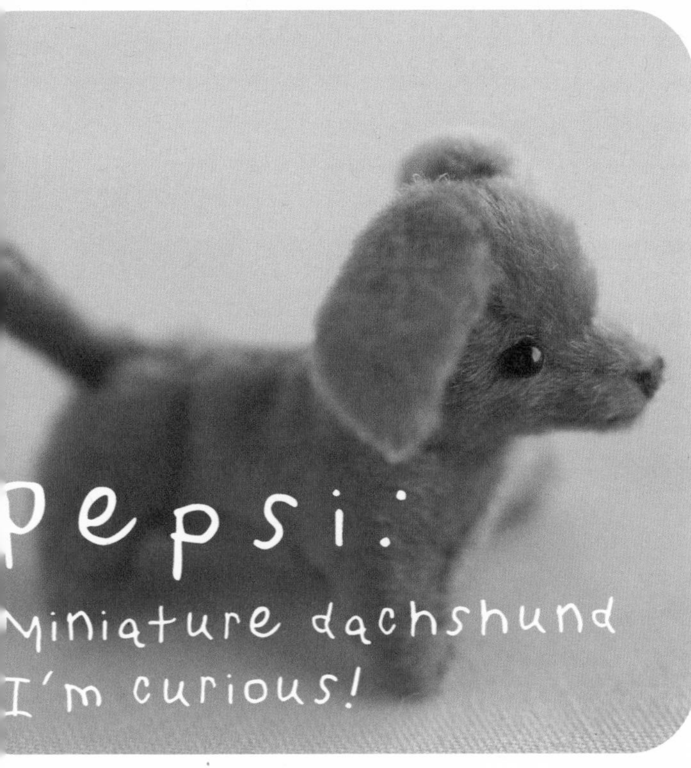
Pepsi:
Miniature dachshund
I'm curious!

Coke:
Miniature dachshund
I'm smart!

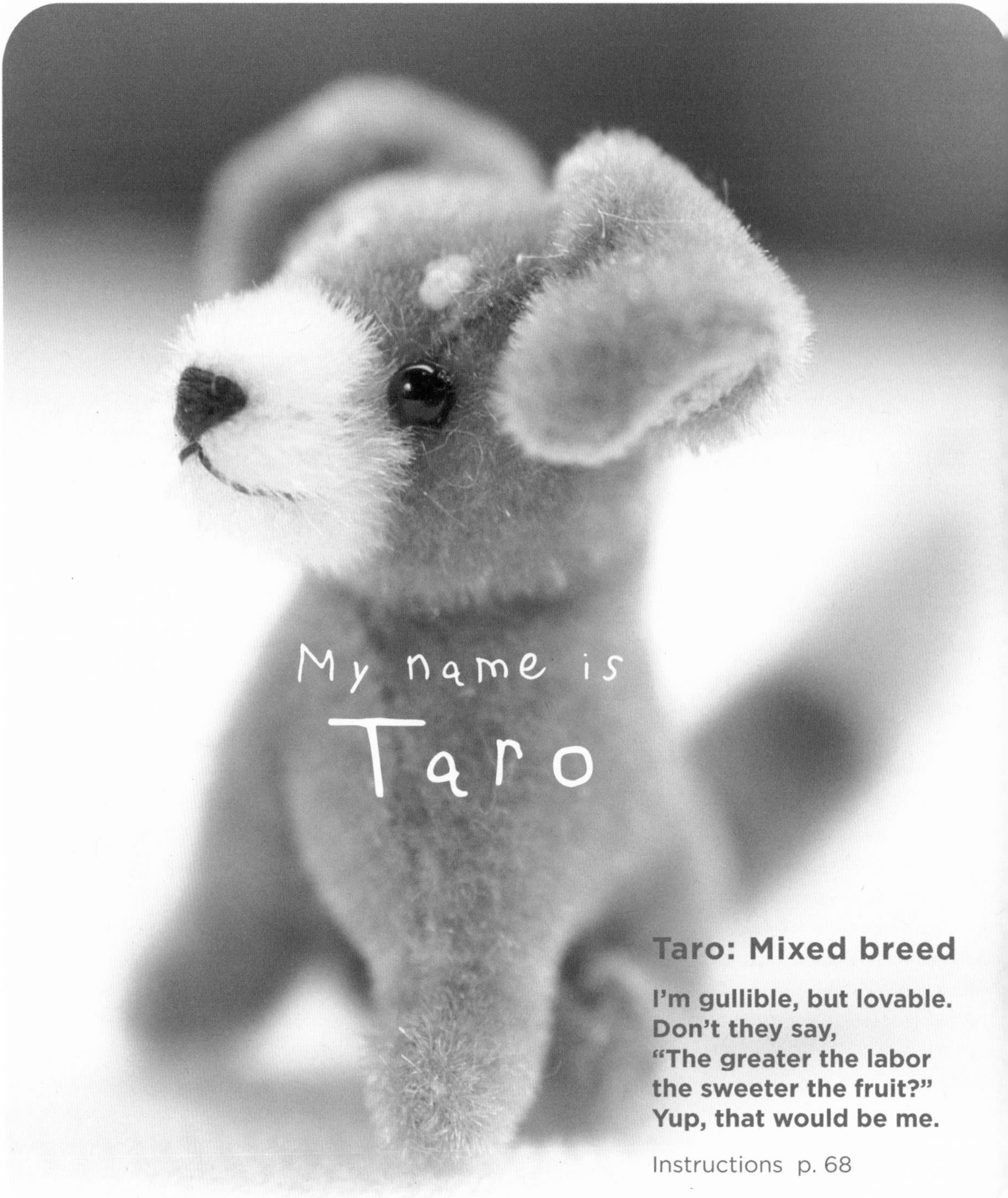

My name is

Taro

Taro: Mixed breed

**I'm gullible, but lovable.
Don't they say,
"The greater the labor
the sweeter the fruit?"
Yup, that would be me.**

Instructions p. 68

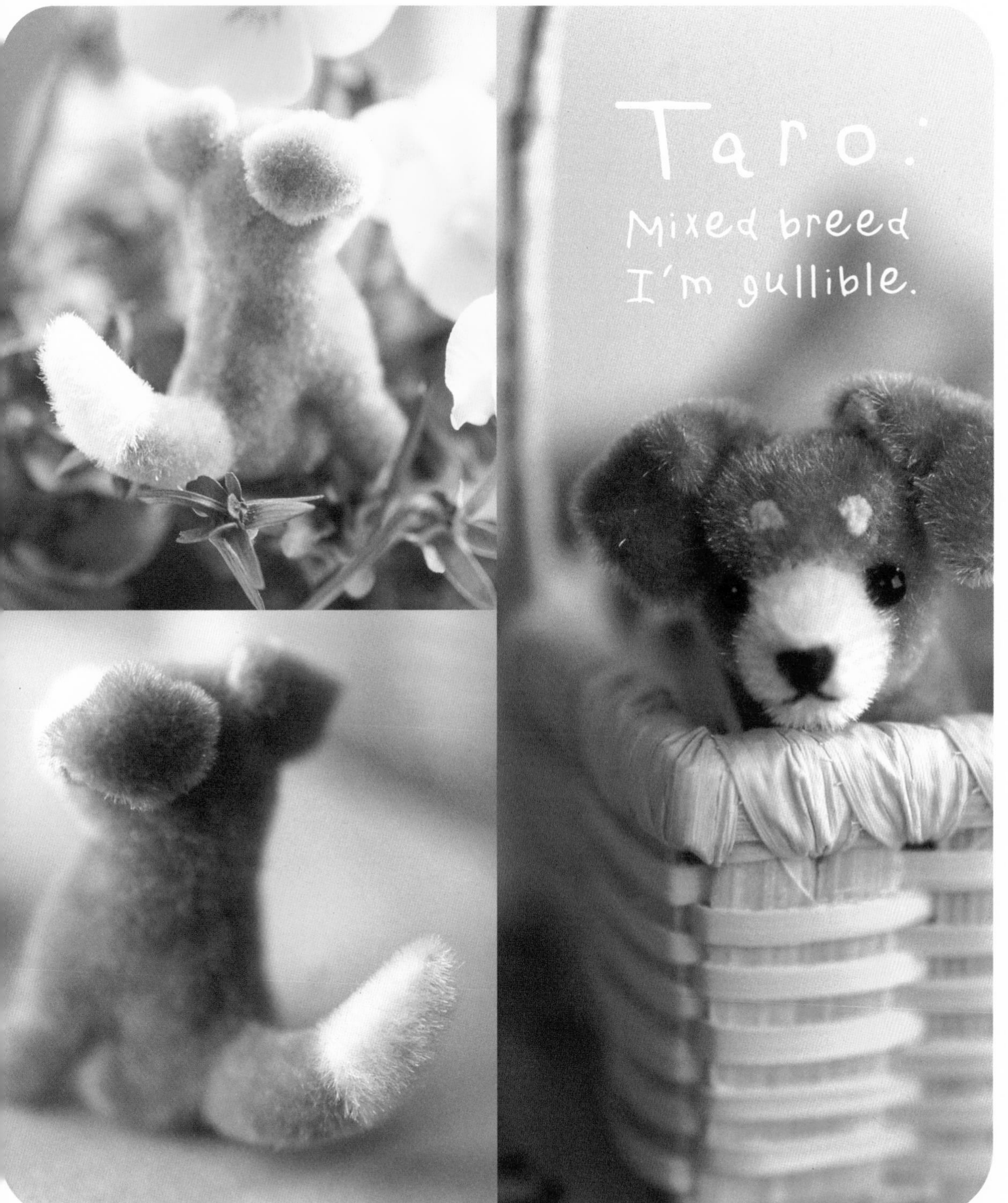
Taro:
Mixed breed
I'm gullible.

My name is
Robin

Robin: Papillon

I'm shy.
I get nervous when
I meet a stranger...
Because, well, I'm shy.

Instructions p. 69

Robin:
Papillon
I'm shy.

We are Jack. Terry. Russell

Jack, Terry, and Russell: Jack Russell Terriers

Three funny brothers.
"I'm hungry." "They just fed us." "Should we beg for more?"

Instructions p. 70

Jack
DOG

Russell
DOG

Terry
DOG

Jack. Terry. Russell:
Jack Russell Terriers
Three funny brothers

My name is

AI

Al: Wirehaired Fox Terrier

**I'm stylish.
I love being brushed.
But I hate taking a bath,
'cause I shrink and look
uncool.**

Instructions p. 71

DOG

A1:

Wirehaired Fox Terrier

I'm stylish.

DOG

My name is
Puddin

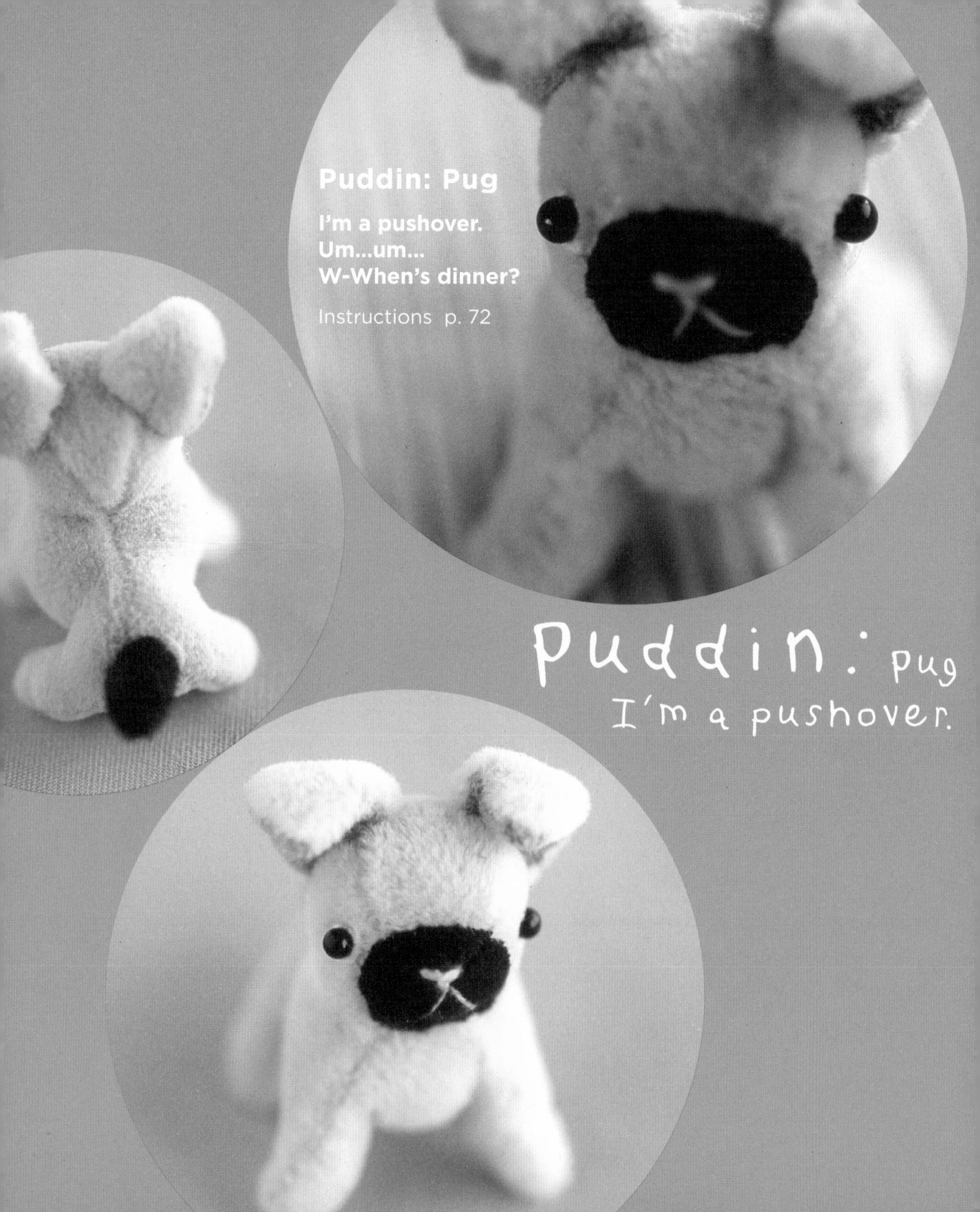

Puddin: Pug

I'm a pushover.
Um...um...
W-When's dinner?

Instructions p. 72

puddin: pug
I'm a pushover.

Daisy:
Shih Tzu
I'm precocious.

Daisy: Shih Tzu

**I'm precocious.
If you put a bow
behind my ear,
I'm even cuter.
Even my squished-in
face is adorable.**

Instructions p. 74

My name is
Daisy

DOG
My name is
Raoul

Raoul:
Miniature Schnauzer
I'm wishy-washy.

Raoul:
Miniature Schnauzer

I do as I please.
Let's take it easy.
Yup, let's just chill.

Instructions p. 75

Snow

puppies

Snow and Ritz: Puppies

They're gonna put bows on us, and take us out for a walk.

Instructions p. 78

Dog Sweet

Ritz

Puppies

**What's this here?
What's over there?
We're super curious.
I mean, everything's
new to us.**

Instructions p. 76

Model dogs

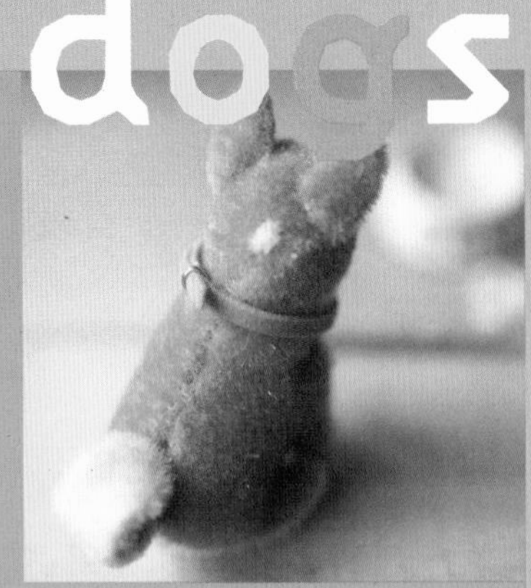

About the models:

I modeled the cute dogs in this section after real dogs. It was fun to create the miniatures while looking at the cute pictures, thinking about the many funny stories the owners told me about them.

Model dog: **Haru**, Shiba Inu

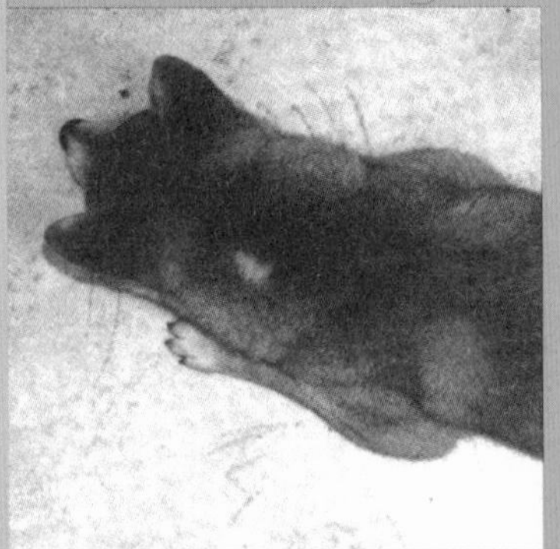

She's a poster girl for a camera shop. She's very laid-back, and has a white spot behind her head.

Model dogs: **Bonzo & Beau**, French Bulldogs

One is black and one is white, so when they sit next to each other, it's like the game Othello. Bonzo is the rambunctious one. I made the area around the mouth pink, and used a pen to draw dots for whiskers.

Model dogs: Jubie & Cookie, Mixed Breed

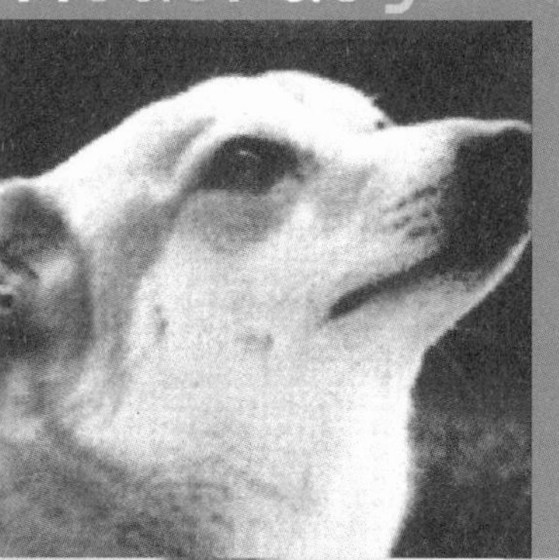

Actually, they're related: Cookie is Jubie's daughter. I heard that when they go for a walk, they walk right next to each other. So cute. I made them here as puppies.

Model dog: Mel, Papillon

She's such a cute girl. She's shy outside, but at home, I hear she acts like a queen. Her back is spotted.

Model dogs

Model dog: Io, Border Collie

Look at his forehead!
It's heart-shaped.
Io is mischievous.

Model dog: Dan, Beagle

His big brown eyes and smiling mouth are too cute. I used glass eyes for this one.

Model dog: Happy, White Terrier

He's very friendly. He loves to go out. Here, he's sticking his tongue out, and firmly standing his ground.

Model dog: Ken, Kaninchen Dachshund

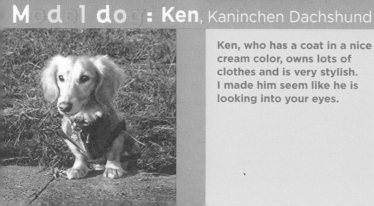

Ken, who has a coat in a nice cream color, owns lots of clothes and is very stylish. I made him seem like he is looking into your eyes.

Everyone together!

The mischievous ones, th
ones that like to be arou
people, the ones that are
always hungry, the shy on
Everyone say cheese!
They're all tiny.
Cute Dogs: 2 1/2 inches h
and about 1/5 an ounce.

How to Make Cute Dogs

All patterns are based on the pattern for Bob. For the variations needed to create the other breeds, there are pointers listed for each dog. These are hand-sewn, and the patterns are all actual-sized patterns. Since the patterns include seam margins, when you sew, you will be sewing about 1/16" (1 to 3 mm) from the edge. You'll need stuffing, thread and stainless steel balls as well as the materials listed for each dog. When estimating the amount of fabric needed, please allow extra.

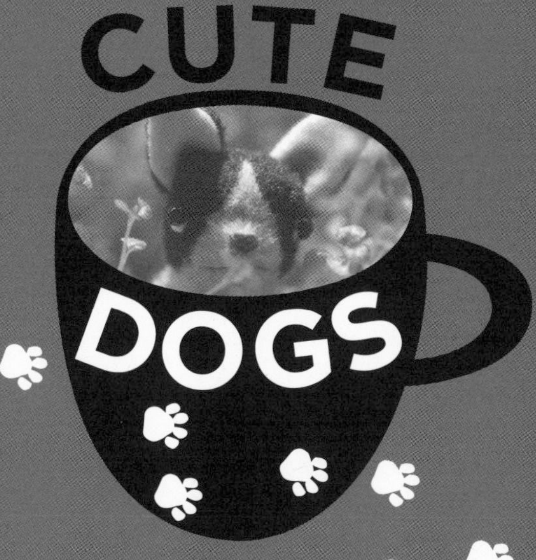
CUTE
DOGS

Materials

Materials needed for making cute dogs are usually available from any store that stocks materials used for making teddy bears.

Miniature fur

Or micro fleece. Soft fabric with pile depth of appx. 1/16" (1 to 3 mm). This fabric doesn't fray easily, and is easy to sew. It also comes in a variety of colors.

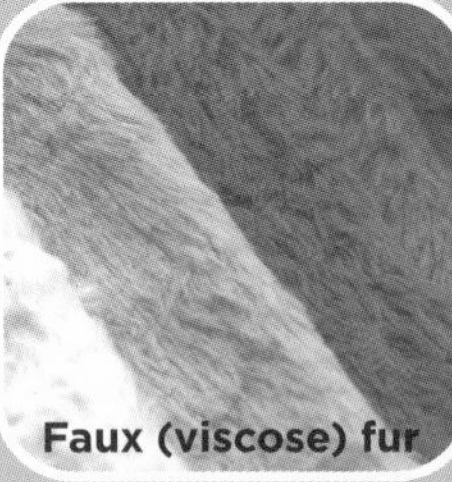

Faux (viscose) fur

Fabric with pile depth of appx. 1/8" (3 to 5 mm). Used when making long-haired dogs. Since faux fur frays more easily compared to fleece (especially when sewing or turning out), treating the raw edges with diluted glue will make it easier to handle.

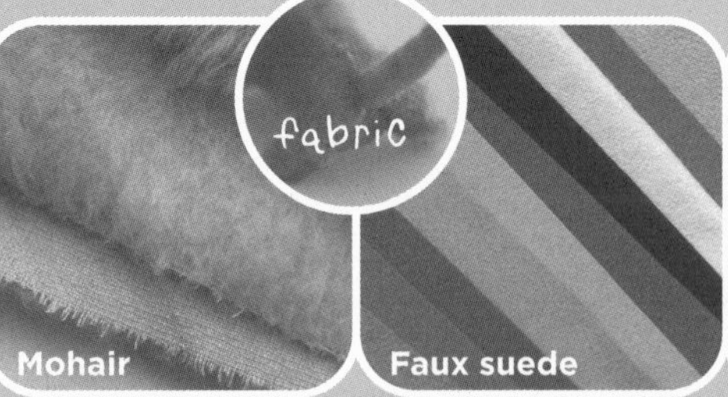
fabric

Mohair

Pile depth is appx. 1/3" (1 cm), and here, I use it for the Pomeranian. Select fabric that is as dense as possible.

Faux suede **Faux suede**

Used for the insides of ears, tongue, and for th dogs' clothes. Thin and easy to handle. There's no need to treat the edges. Comes in a variety of colors. There are different types such as ultr and micro suede, and I've sorted them based c the color.

FUJIX
MONOCOLOR
#60

Transparent nylon thread (for plain seams)

Can be used with any type of fabric, and since it is transparent, it won't spoil the look. Although tricky to use at first, it's very convenient.

Polyester thread No. 60 (for plain seams)

Strong and flexible. Easy to use; recommended for those who have a hard time using the transparent nylon thread.

Embroidery thread, machine thread No. 50 (black)

Used for noses and mouths. I use machine thread No. 50 (black) that has a slight sheen to it. Of course, embroidery thread works too.

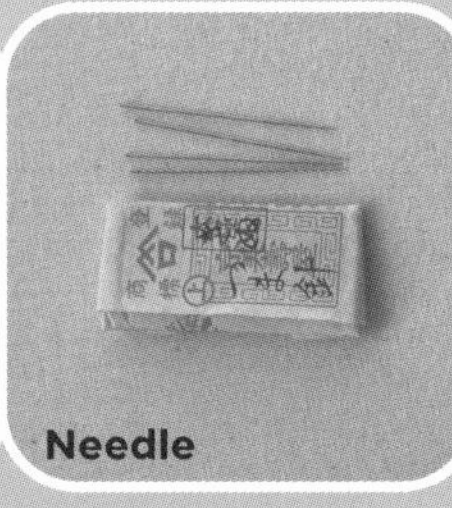

Needle

Thin needles. I use a fine silk thread needle.

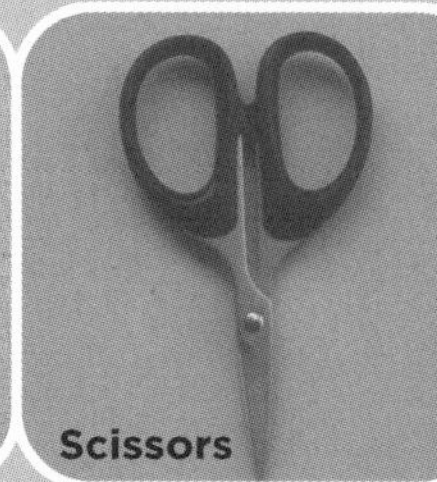

Scissors

A sharp pair with narr blades.

Basic Sewing

Since the cute dogs are small, they're all hand-sewn.

Pointers!

Use half-backstitch for stitching pieces of fabric together, and use 1/16" (1 to 3 mm) stitches. At the beginning and at the end of the stitches, always go back one stitch. Make a French knot at the end, scoop up one stitch and draw the thread, hiding the knot.

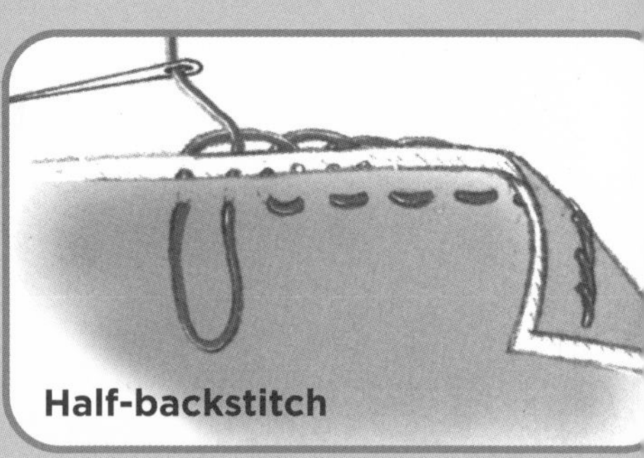

Half-backstitch

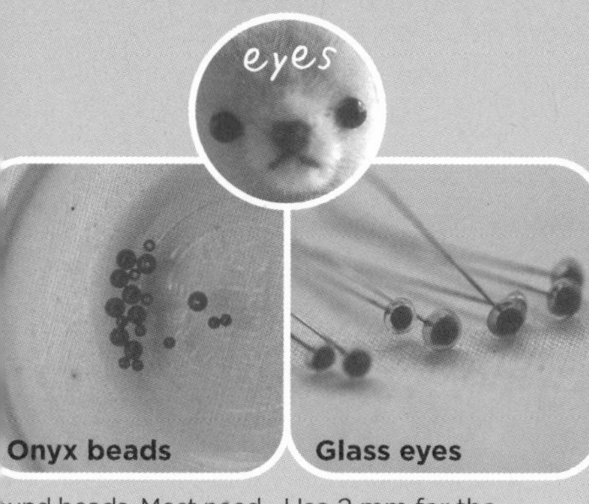
eyes

Onyx beads

ound beads. Most need
mm beads (for the
ll Terrier, use 1.5 mm).
owever, since sizes
ry depending on the
and, use whatever's
ailable, and enjoy how
e expression changes
epending on slight
riations in size.

Glass eyes

Use 2 mm for the puppies, Ritz and Snow. Also, when you use glass eyes, it makes them look interesting. Loop the wire with a pair of pliers, insert, and secure by sewing.

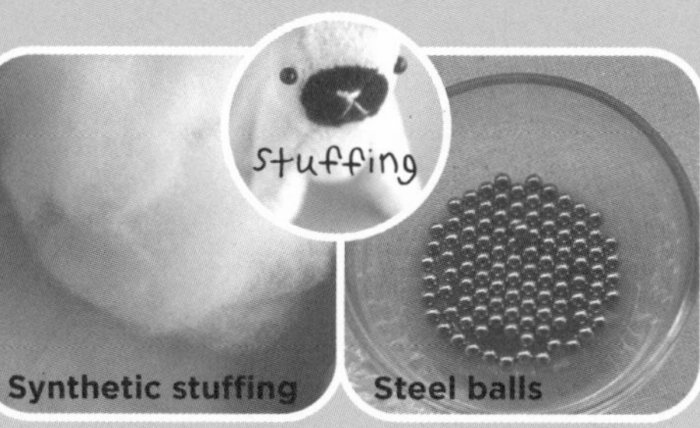
stuffing

Synthetic stuffing

Pull off small clumps and squeeze into little pieces before stuffing.

Steel balls

Small balls made of stainless steel. In order to give the dogs stability and weight, I wrap about 15 to 20 balls into the stuffing. I use small ones, appx. 3 mm in diameter.

ボンド
木工用
水性

Wood glue

Coat the raw edges of easily frayed fabric with diluted glue. This makes fabric easier to work with.

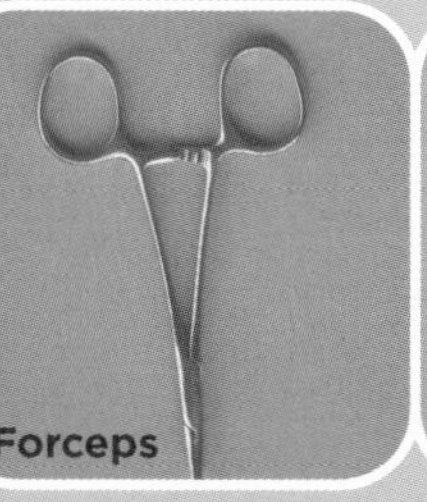

Forceps

Tweezers

though forceps are a surgical tool, they're
ry convenient when turning out pieces or
hen stuffing the cute dog. If forceps aren't
ailable, use marking pins or a set of tweezers.

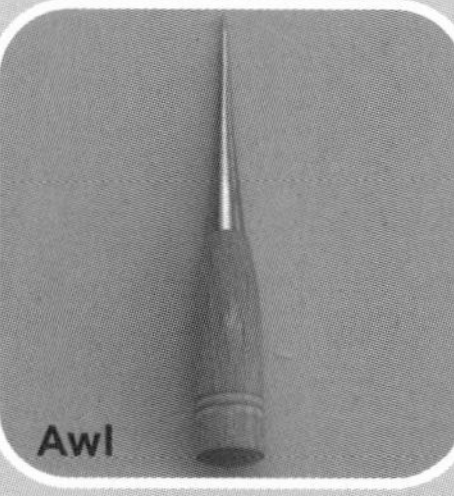

Awl

Thin type used for crafting. Used for punching holes where eyes are to be placed, or when pulling out pile that got caught in the seams.

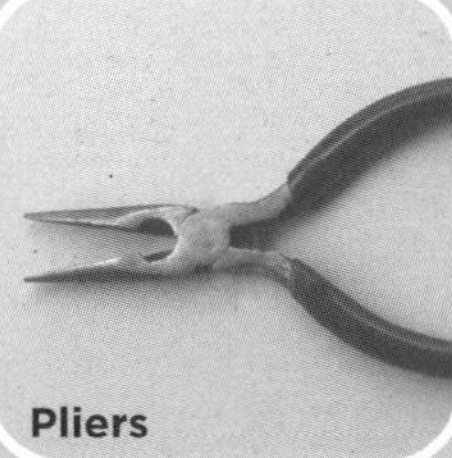

Pliers

Used when cutting or bending wires for glass eyes or when making a latch for the collar.

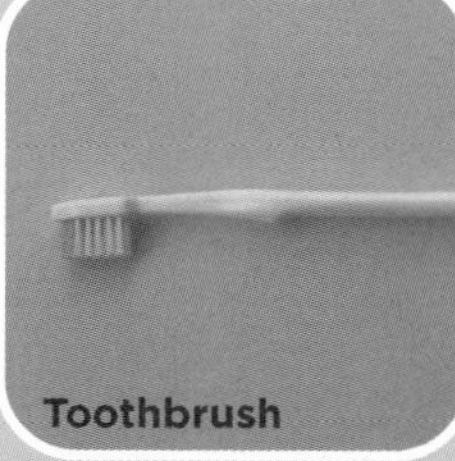

Toothbrush

Used for brushing.

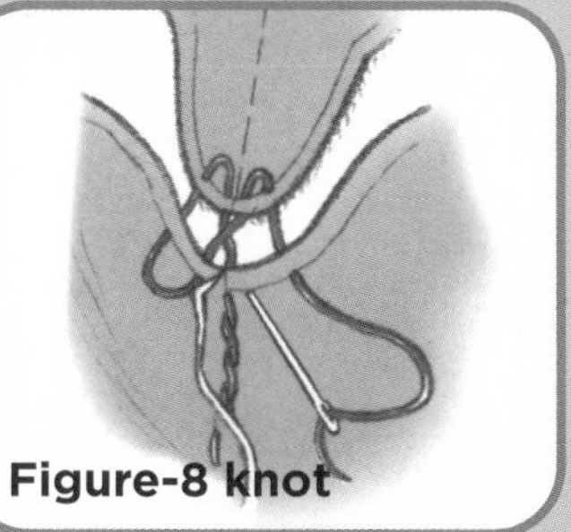

Figure-8 knot

For stitching the tip of the snout, under the jaw, and stitching together two edges of fabric, use a figure-8 knot. This way, the pieces will stay aligned. Use smaller stitches for the snout and the legs since they tend to unravel when turning out the fabric or adding stuffing.

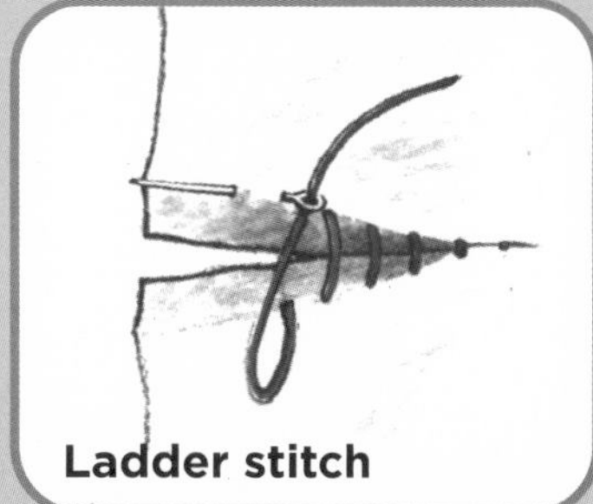

Ladder stitch

When closing an opening, take the same stitch alternately through abutted fabric. While pushing in the stuffing with the needle to keep it inside, sew the fabric together so that the thread forms a reversed "C."

Instruction Pointers

I'm sure there are various ways of making the cute dogs, but I'd like to list some helpful tips.

Placing the pattern and cutting the fabric

Take note of the grain (or fur) direction. There's an arrow on each pattern to indicate the grain line. Also, when there are 2 separate pieces for the torso and the ears, reverse the fabric so that the pieces are symmetrical. The patterns include seam margins. When placing a pattern on the reverse side, follow the pattern to mark the fabric then cut.
For those that use fleece, sew appx. 1 to 2 mm from the raw edges. For the legs, keep appx. 2 mm of seam margin when sewing. Sometimes I cut the fabric directly without tracing the pattern. It's impossible to make them exactly alike, and besides, I think it's fun that they are all different.

Treating the raw edges of faux fur and mohair

Since they tend to fray, keep larger seam margins (2 to 3 mm). Treating the edges of the fabric will make it easier to work with. Dilute wood glue with a small amount of water, coat the edges with a brush, and let dry.

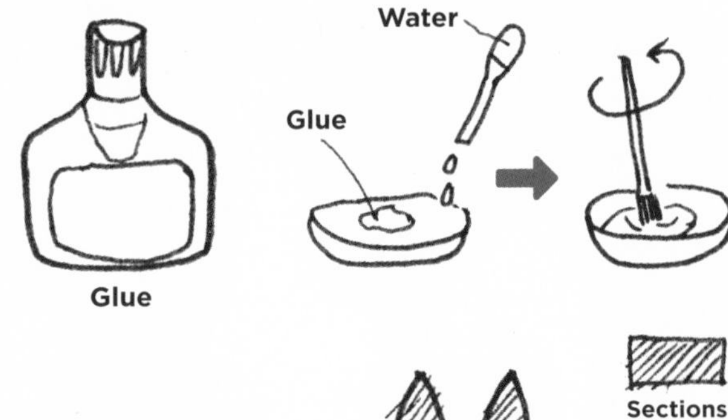
Water
Glue
Glue

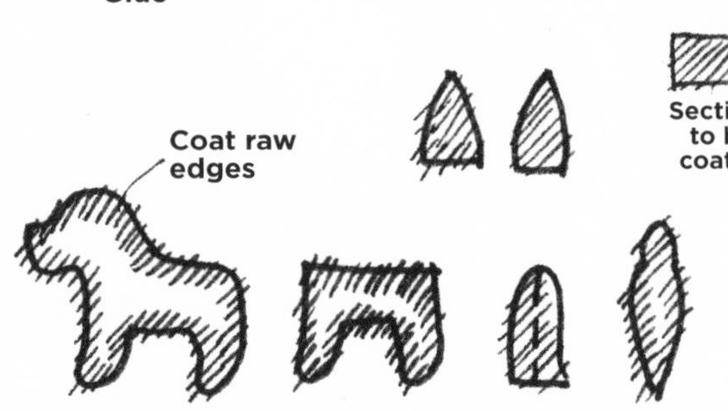
Coat raw edges
Sections to be coated

Small parts

Since the white parts for the eyes and eyebrows are very small, I cut them right before attaching so as not to lose them. Refer to page 58 on how to cut them out.

Dogs' coat patterns

The coat patterns such as patches are sewn on like appliqués. Since they are so small, it's tough to stitch together the pooch's patterns—especially curves—with the fabric inside out. Like an appliqué, place the pattern piece over the body fabric, and use small cross-stitches to lock in the edges of the pattern piece. Now there are 2 layers of fabric which makes it hard to turn out, so cut off the section of the fabric underneath the pattern piece leaving appx. 2 mm of seam margin.

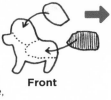

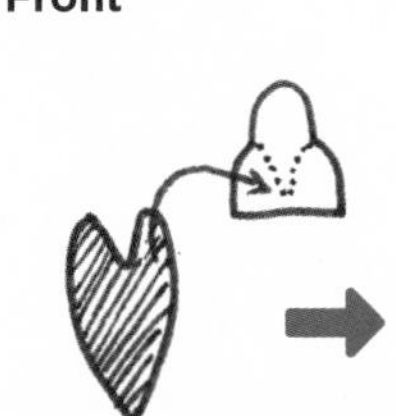
Front

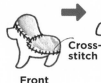

Front

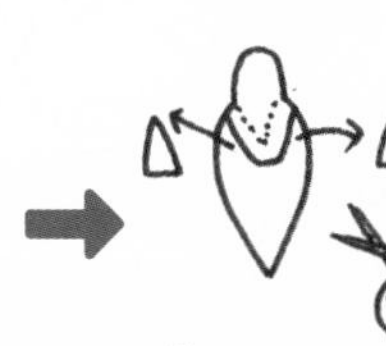
Reverse

How to make floppy ears

After attaching ears, bend ear by threading from point A to point B (where you want the ear to bend). In style (1), sew together both sides of the folded ear, and style (2), sew the ear onto the head. Afterwards, bring the thread back to point A, make a French knot, take up one stitch, then cut the thread.

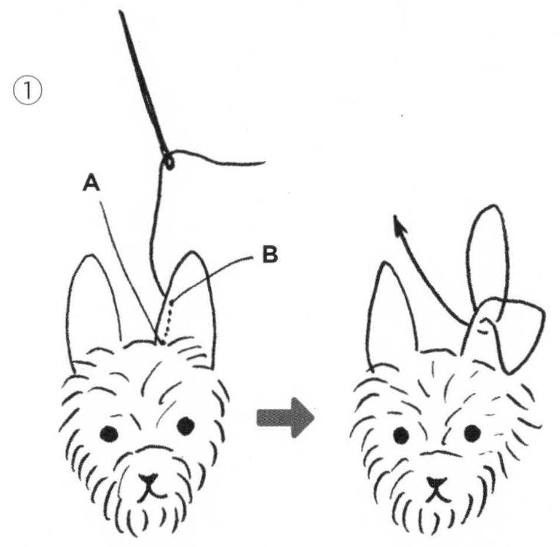

①
A
B

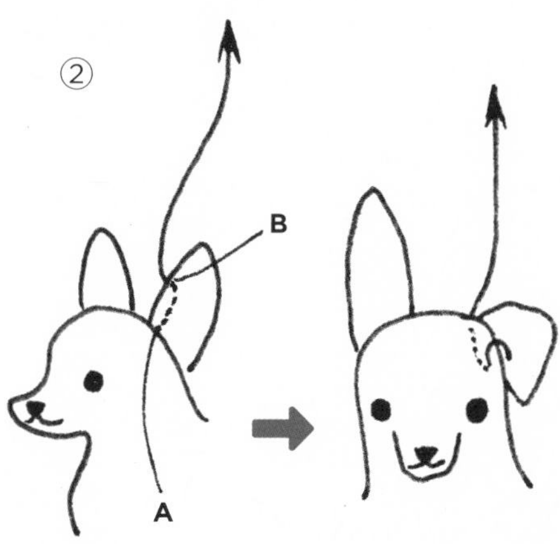

②
B
A

53

How to make a curved tail

Stitch top and bottom pieces together, then sew sides A and B, with the gather on side B.

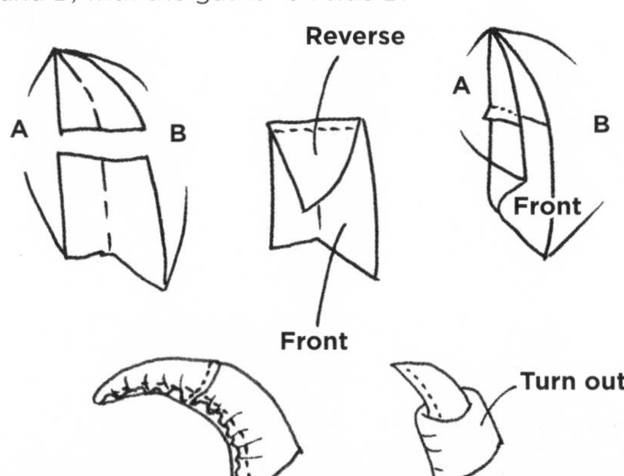

A
B
Reverse
Front
A
B
Front
Turn out

Pointers!

Finishing

Pull out any fur that got caught in the seams by using an awl or needle and brush with a toothbrush. Careful finishing makes all the difference.

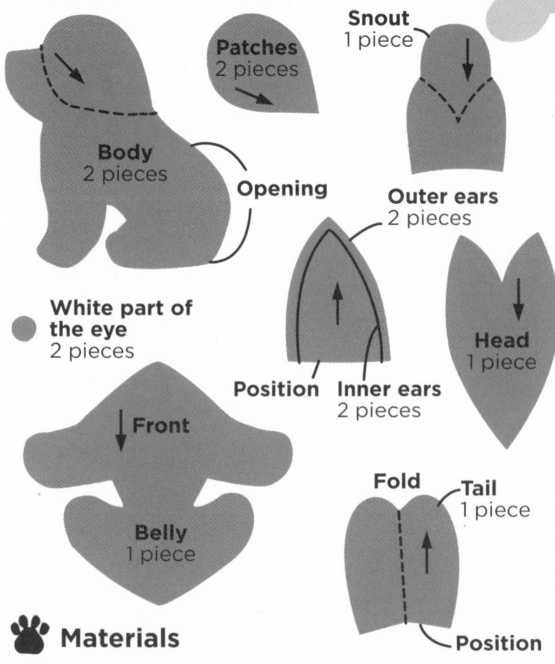
Body
2 pieces
Patches
2 pieces
Snout
1 piece
Opening
Outer ears
2 pieces
White part of the eye
2 pieces
Head
1 piece
Position
Inner ears
2 pieces
Front
Belly
1 piece
Fold
Tail
1 piece
Position

CUTE DOGS

Bob: Boston Terrier (p. 6)

He is comical, lovable, and has character. His wide-spaced eyes with upturned glance seem to be pleading for something.

Pointers!
Squished-in snout
Big eyes

Materials

Body, belly, snout: miniature fur/fleece (beige)
Patches, head, outer ears, tail: miniature fur/fleece (black)
Inner ears: micro suede (pink)
Pupils: onyx beads
Whites of eyes: ultra suede (white)

Make the patterns

Lay a thick piece of tracing paper on the patterns, secure it so that it won't move, then trace the patterns with a pencil. For those with overlapping patterns such as outer ears and inner ears, trace patterns separately, write down on each the grain line, opening, names of parts, and the number of pieces needed. Cut out the patterns with a pair of sharp scissors following the line.

Mark the fabric

Lay patterns next to each other on the reverse side of the fabric, paying attention to the grain direction. Mark the fabric with a fine ball-point pen or pencil. Don't forget to flip the pattern for symmetrical parts such as the chest, patches and ears. Also mark the fabric with notches for the openings, etc.

Cut the fabric

With a pair of narrow, sharp scissors, cut little by little so you don't cut the pile.

Beige
Black
Pink
Miniature fur/Fleece
Micro suede
?

Instructions
Bob

Sew

❶ Sew the patch pieces onto the main body pieces as if sewing on an appliqué.

Lay the patch piece on the main body, and sew it on by using small cross-stitches (appx. 1 mm apart). Pull the thread towards the inside so that the reverse of the fabric on top won't show.
Where there are two layers of fabric, cut off the fabric underneath (here, in beige) appx. 3 mm from the seam (you won't be able to turn out the fabric if it's too thick.)
Attach the snout to the head, and cut off the underside fabric there, too.

Pointers!

When you have complex patterns and shapes, treat them like appliqués. Since the fabric is furry, the seam will be hidden, and it won't show very much.

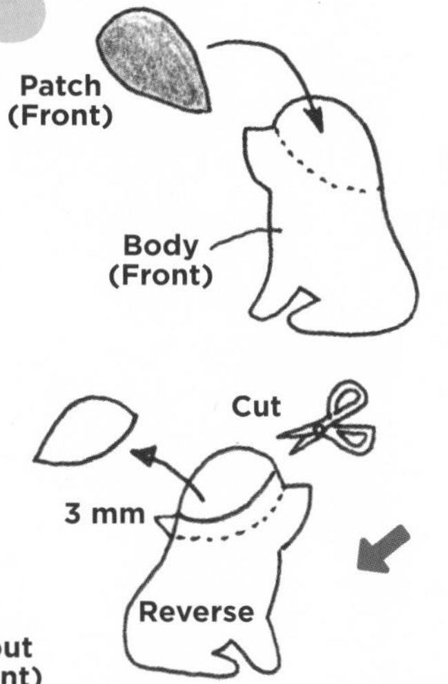

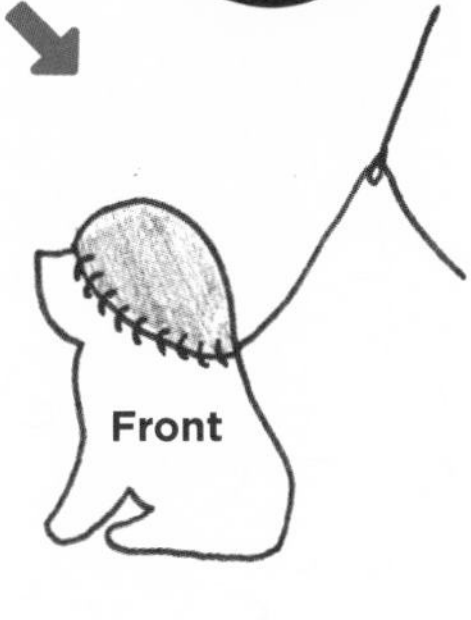

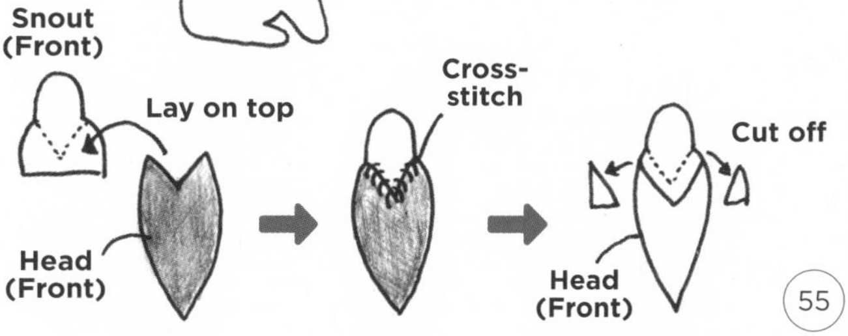

❷ Sew together each piece.
(Use half-backstitches for sewing pieces together and ladder stitches when closing an opening.)

First, place the front sides of the body pieces facing each other, then sew under the jaw from point A to point B. When you reach point B, which is the tip of the snout, firmly secure the head piece using a figure-8 knot. Since the snout section has three layers of fabric and can tear easily, make the figure-8 several times to reinforce it.

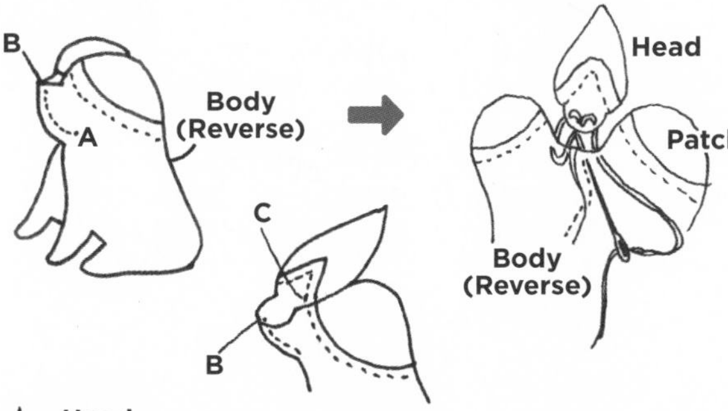

Sew the snout piece to the body from point B to point C on one side, and add approximately 2 more stitches at point C to reinforce it.

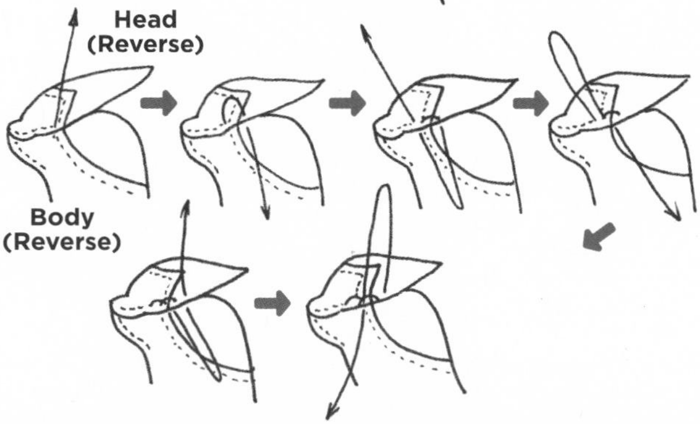

Patch (Front)
Body (Front)
Front
Cut
3 mm
Reverse
Snout (Front)
Lay on top
Cross-stitch
Cut off
Head (Front)
Head (Front)
B
A
Body (Reverse)
Head
Patch
C
B
Body (Reverse)
Head (Reverse)
Body (Reverse)

Sew

Continue to sew to point D, then sew the other side from point B on the snout, back through point D to point E.

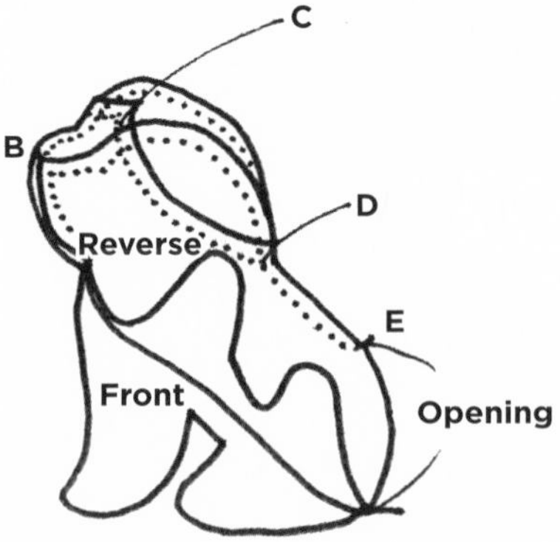

Sew together the belly piece and the body piece starting from point A under the jaw. Sew together by gradually easing the fabric so that each point matches up (such as points A under the jaw, points F under the arm, points G at the hind leg joint, and points H at the rear).
By gathering the fabric, you can achieve fullness for the body and the head.

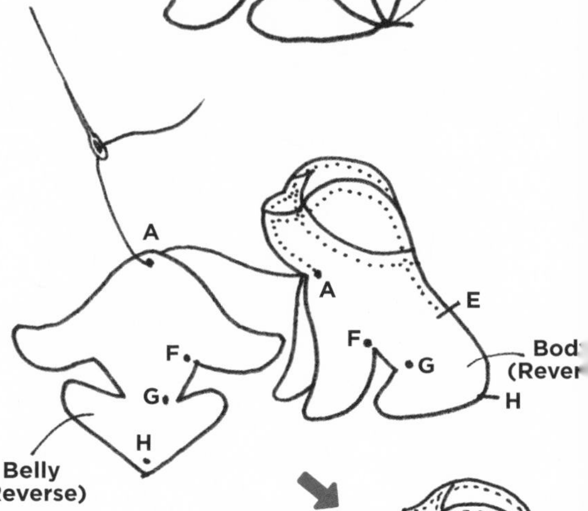

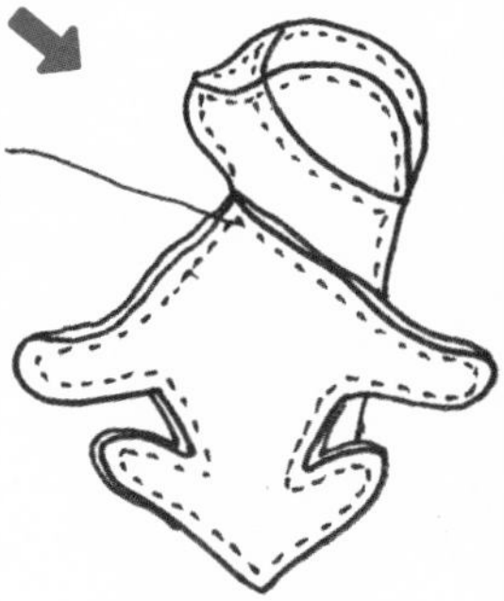

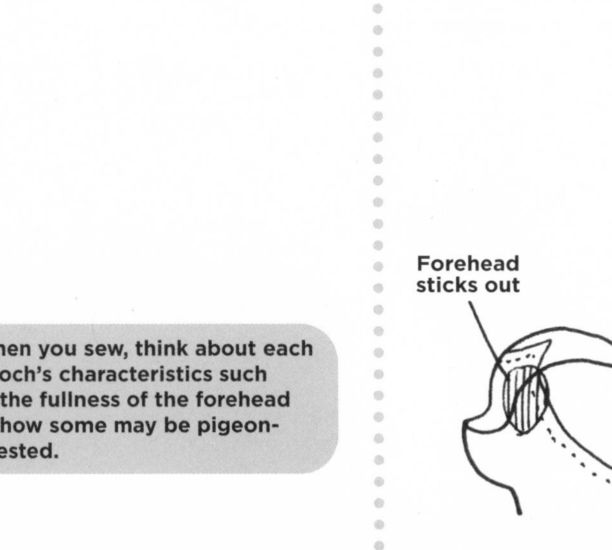
Forehead
sticks out

Pointers!

When you sew, think about each pooch's characteristics such as the fullness of the forehead or how some may be pigeon-chested.

Instructions Bob

Turn it out

'urn out little by little through the opening. Don't try o do it all at once; go slowly. Once you get it as far as ›ossible by hand, use forceps or a pin to turn it out by ›ushing out the legs and the tip of the snout. For delicate ›arts, scoop the fabric with a marking pin to pull it out. 3e careful not to tear it.

Body (Reverse)
Opening
Insert forceps and slowly turn out

Scoop out from the front

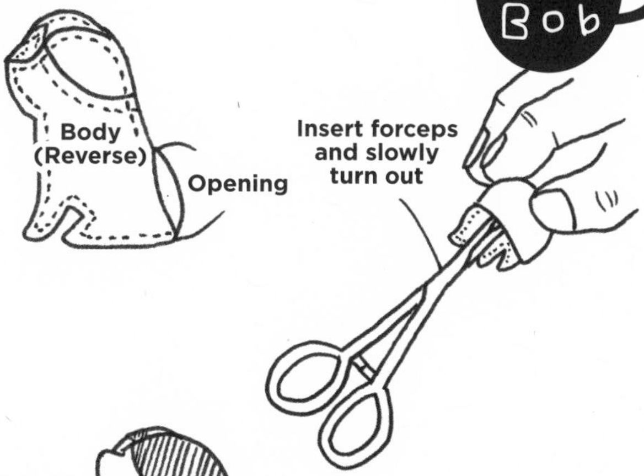

Stuffing

ear off small portions of stuffing little by little. Starting vith the snout, stuff it gradually by using forceps or a set of tweezers. Unless you stuff it firmly, it'll be hard to give : an expression later on. After firmly stuffing the head, tuff the legs, then the body. When stuffing the body, vrap approximately 15 to 20 stainless steel balls in the tuffing to give it some weight. This way, it's stable and as presence.

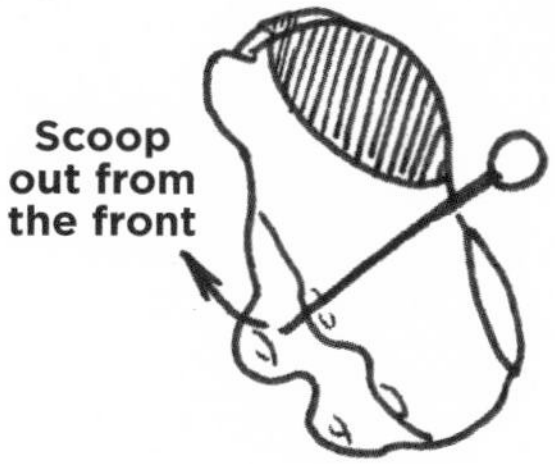

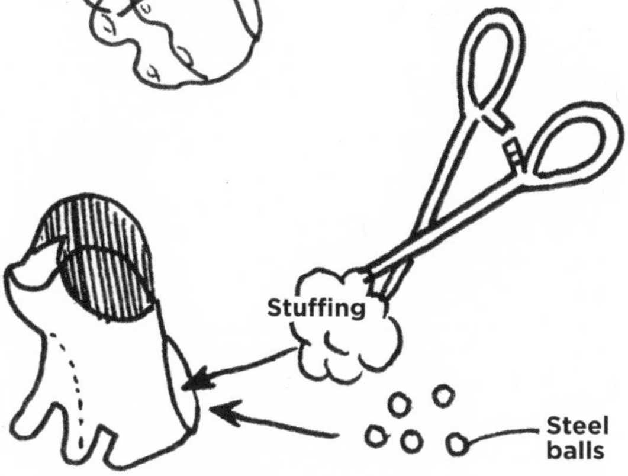

Stuffing
Steel balls

Making the face

'his is the fun part!
Make any face you like.

❶ Making the nose and mouth

'rim the fur around the nose and the mouth a little.

ısert needle where the ear joins the head, and pull out t the tip of the snout.

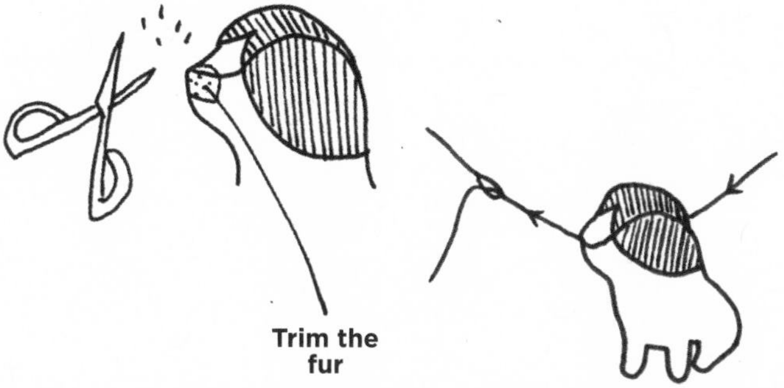

Trim the fur

Instructions
Bob

Making the face

First, sew the outline of the nose, then fill it in with straight stitches. To finish, pull the thread out where the ear on the opposite side joins the head, make a French knot, and scoop up one stitch before cutting the thread.

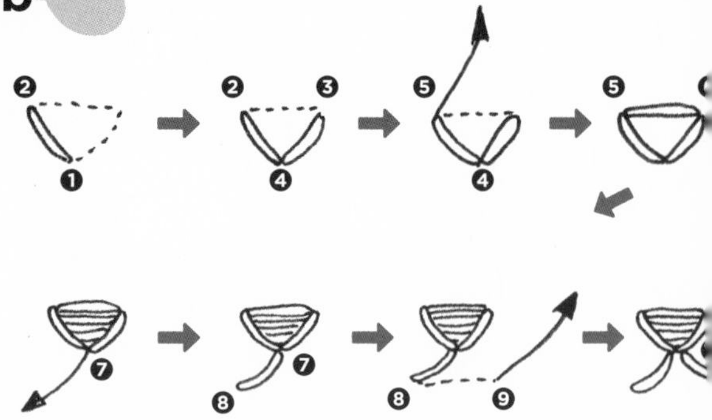

❷ Attach the eyes

First, the whites of the eyes. Since it's difficult to cut out small parts when holding the fabric, cut out the pieces with a little extra allowance, impale it on a needle or a marking pin, then cut off the excess.

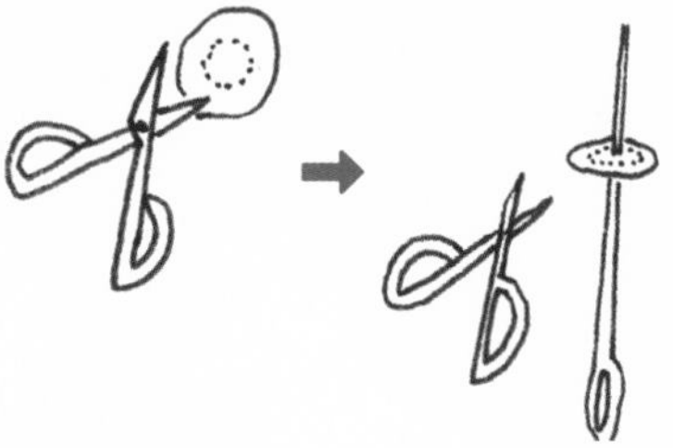

Next, the pupils. Place the white part of the eye to where you would like the eye situated, then insert the needle into the fabric where the ear joins the head and pull out of the head through the center of the white of the eye. Thread an onyx bead and sew it on. Thread it through a couple of times and secure it firmly so that the hole doesn't show. It makes it even better if you sew the onyx bead towards the upper part of the white of the eye.

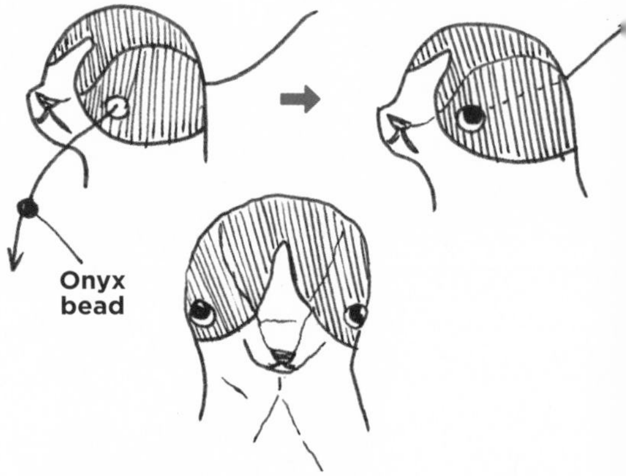

Onyx bead

Attach Ears and Tail

The pattern for the inner ears is smaller so that the ears can curve inward. With both pieces reverse-side out, stitch the edges together, then turn out. After folding in the edges of the opening a little, use cross-stitches to close the opening.
For Bob, since the ears and the tail are narrow, don't stuff them.

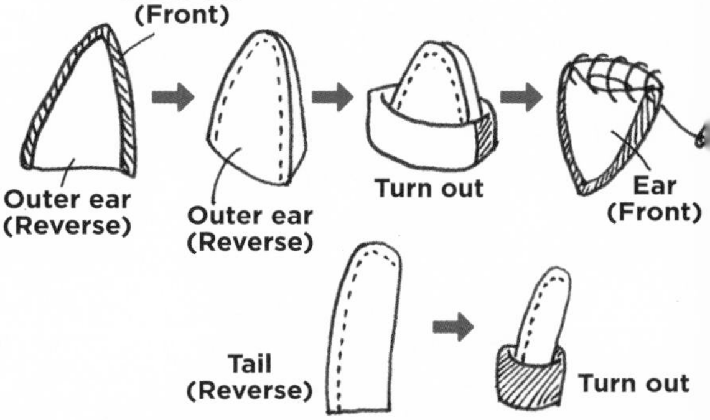

Outer ear (Front)
Outer ear (Reverse)
Outer ear (Reverse)
Turn out
Ear (Front)
Tail (Reverse)
Turn out

Instructions Bob

Attach the Ears and the Tail

)ecide on where to put the ears. First sew point A, then ecure point B, then sew from A to B in a curved line, naking the ear concave.

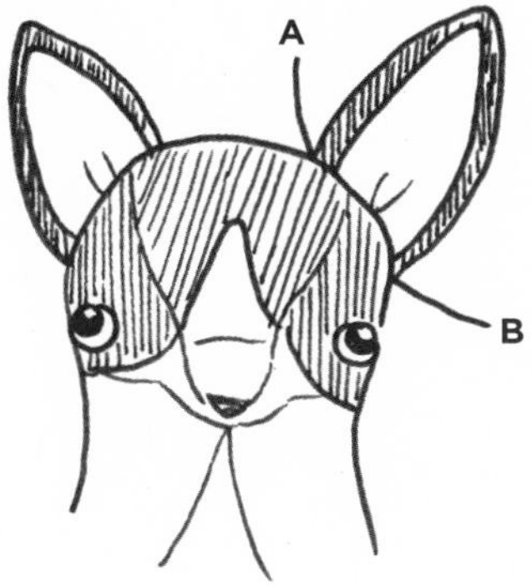

Jext, attach the tail. Close the opening in the back using adder stitches, leaving enough opening to insert the tail. Vhen cross-stitching on the tail, add stuffing little by little hrough the opening to shape the rear end and the body.

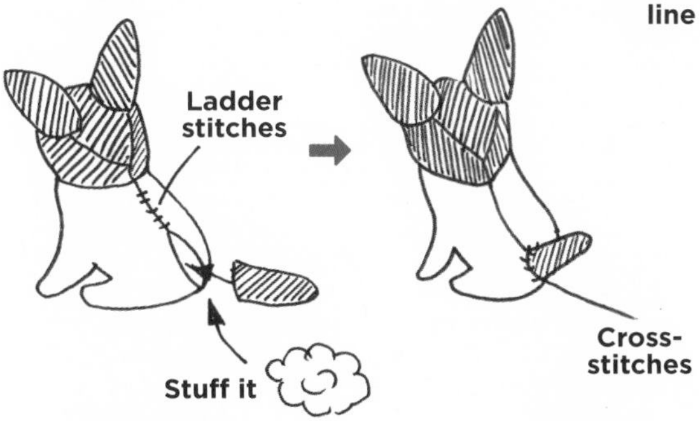

A

B

Stitch in a curved line

Ladder stitches

Stuff it

Cross-stitches

Finishing

'o create Bob's squished-in look, create wrinkles by adding an inside stitch.
;tart from the back of the head. Pull the thread through he base of the snout and back out the back of the head. Aake the tip of the snout point upward. Next, insert the ieedle in the same starting point, out under the jaw, up hrough the bridge of the snout and back down again hrough the same spot under the jaw. Make a French knot inder the jaw, and scoop up one stitch before cutting the hread.

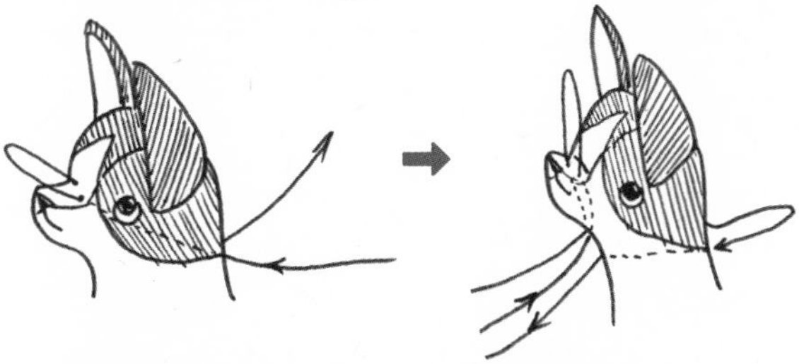

Vere you able to make a squished-in snout? Lastly, brush he stuffed animal with a toothbrush. Pull out the pile rom under the seam, brush the coat with a toothbrush, ind you're done.

Instructions Lulu

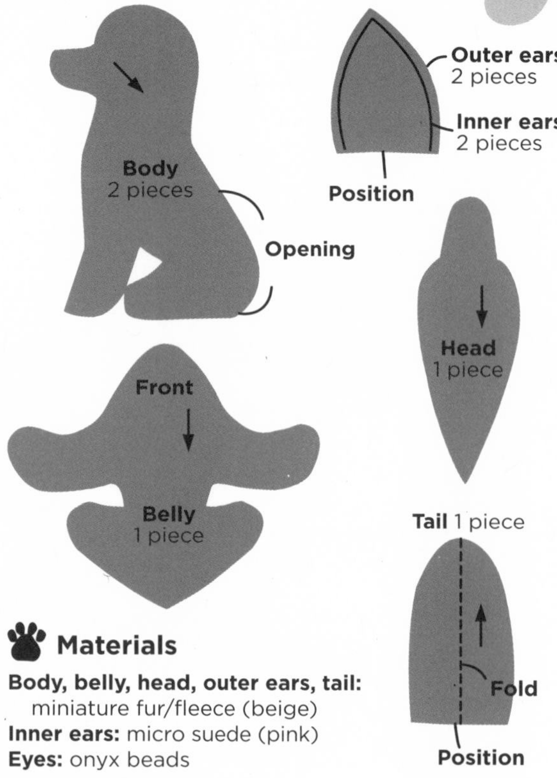
Body
2 pieces
Opening
Outer ears
2 pieces
Inner ears
2 pieces
Position
Head
1 piece
Front
Belly
1 piece
Tail 1 piece
Fold
Position

Materials

Body, belly, head, outer ears, tail: miniature fur/fleece (beige)
Inner ears: micro suede (pink)
Eyes: onyx beads

Pointers

Don't stuff the tail.

CUTE DOGS

Lulu

Lulu: Chihuahua (p. 12)

Chihuahuas give us an impression that they are always shivering. I feel like telling them, "It's OK!"

Pointers!
Large ears
Rounded forehead

Instructions
Chibi

Opening

Body
2 pieces

Outer ears
2 pieces

Inner ears
2 pieces

Position

Fold

Tail
1 piece

Position

Front

Belly
1 piece

Head
1 piece

Materials

ody, belly, head, outer ears, tail:
mohair (golden brown)

nner ears: micro suede (pink)

yes: onyx beads

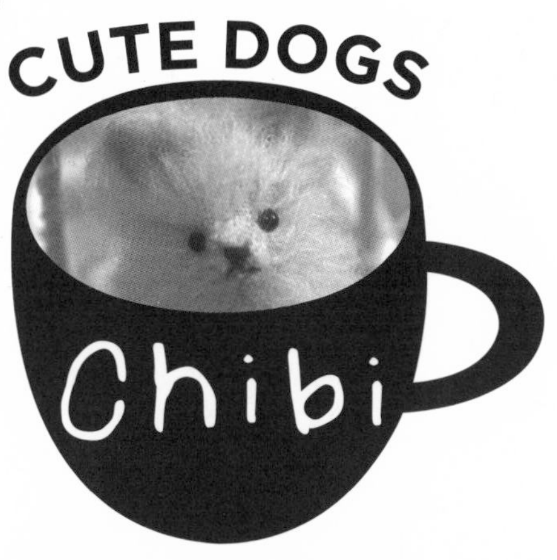
CUTE DOGS
Chibi

Chibi: Pomeranian (p. 14)

Pomeranians are fluffy, like cotton candy. My heart melts when they look at me with those lovely round eyes.

Pointers!
Fluffy fur
Large curling tail

Note

ou can achieve the fluffiness of a Pomeranian by using ong-hair mohair. Use fine-textured mohair with appx. 1/2" 1.2 cm) long hair. Here, I used antique-looking wool mohair. Cut the fabric little by little so as not to cut the pile. Once ou're done cutting, trim away the pile at the tip of the nout, feet and at seam margins. Mohair fabric is thicker han mini fur due to its pile length, and it's harder to turn ut the fabric. Be careful not to pull out the hair.

Curled Tail

o make a curled tail, fold lightly along the placement line nd sew the opening closed. Don't stuff the tail. Close the opening on the back part way. Insert the tail o that the seam faces upward. Once you finish stuffing he rear, cross-stitch the tail in place. Without cutting the hread, pull out where the tail joins the back, insert the eedle through the tip of the tail (point A), then insert it gain where the tail joins the back, thread through the ear, and secure it with a knot.

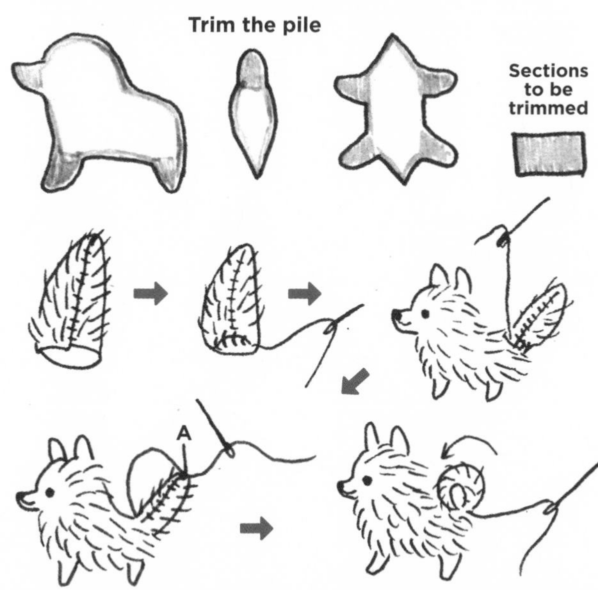
Trim the pile
Sections to be trimmed
A

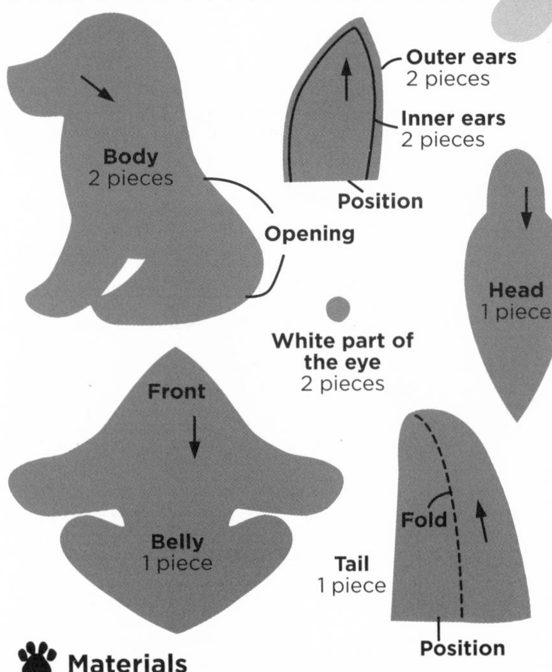
Body
2 pieces
Opening
Outer ears
2 pieces
Inner ears
2 pieces
Position
Head
1 piece
White part of the eye
2 pieces
Front
Belly
1 piece
Fold
Tail
1 piece
Position

Materials

Body, belly, head, outer ears, tail: mini fur (black)
Inner ears: ultra suede (smoky pink)
Whites of eyes: ultra suede (white)
Pupils: onyx beads

CUTE DOGS
Love

Love: Labrador Retriever (p. 16)

Since his coat is black, I added whites of the eyes to give him a saucy look. Although a real black Lab is large and is a very cool dog, as a miniature pup, this is more like it.

Pointer!
Saucy eyes

Eyes

To give him a fun-loving expression, sew on the onyx bead pupils a little left of center. This will allow the white part of the eyes to show, creating a sidelong glance.

Pointers

Whites of eyes: Refer to page 58
Droopy ears: Refer to Instruction Pointer 5
Tail: Stuff the tail: Refer to Instruction Pointer 6

Point close-up

Instructions
Mandy

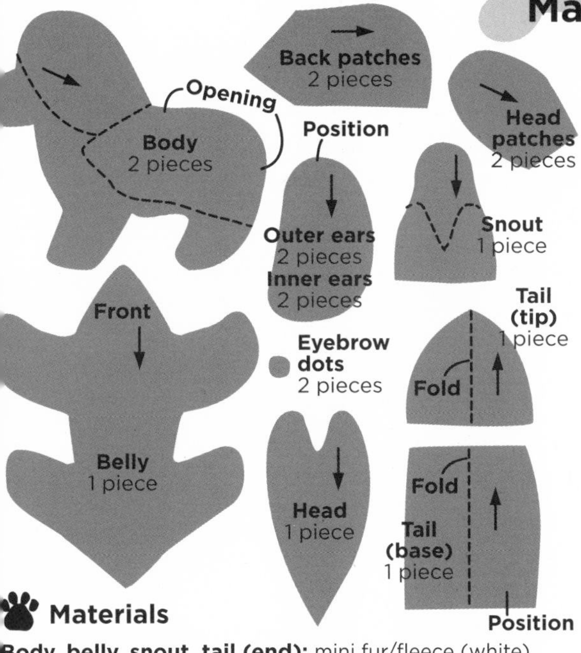

Back patches
2 pieces
Head patches
2 pieces
Opening
Body
2 pieces
Position
Outer ears
2 pieces
Inner ears
2 pieces
Snout
1 piece
Front
Tail (tip)
1 piece
Eyebrow dots
2 pieces
Fold
Belly
1 piece
Head
1 piece
Fold
Tail (base)
1 piece
Position

Materials

Body, belly, snout, tail (end): mini fur/fleece (white)
Head, patches on the head, outer ears: mini fur/fleece (brown)
Patches on the back, tail (base): mini fur/fleece (black)
Inner ears, eyebrow dots: ultra suede (beige)
Eyes: onyx beads

CUTE DOGS

Mandy

Mandy: Beagle (p. 18)

Use three colors to make a beagle. I think she looks good with a bandana instead of a collar.

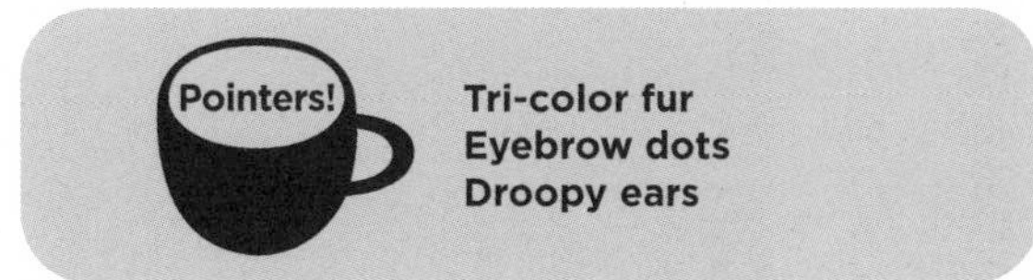

Pointers!
Tri-color fur
Eyebrow dots
Droopy ears

Eyebrow Dot

Insert the needle from the back of the head, and pull the thread out where you would like to put an eyebrow dot. If you insert the needle in the middle of the eyebrow dot and draw the thread towards the back of the head, the eyebrow dot will sink in a little, making it shrink slightly. Make a French knot to secure, scoop up one stitch, then cut the thread.

Pointers

Patches: Refer to Instruction Pointer 4
Tail: Stuff the tail.

Two-Color Tail

Sew together by placing both the tail piece (end) and the tail piece (base) reverse-side out.

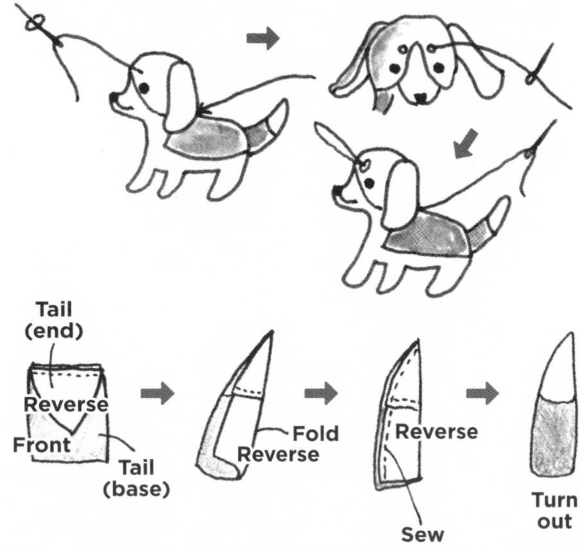

Tail (end)
Reverse
Front
Tail (base)
Fold
Reverse
Reverse
Sew
Turn out

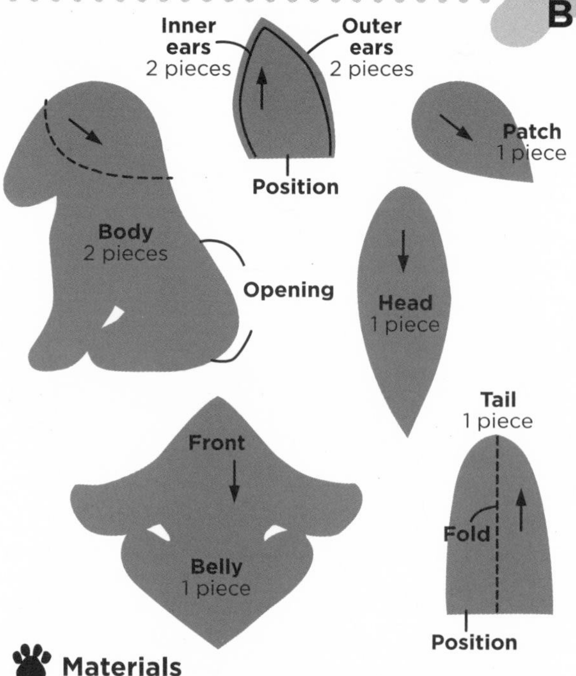
Inner ears
2 pieces
Outer ears
2 pieces
Patch
1 piece
Position
Body
2 pieces
Opening
Head
1 piece
Tail
1 piece
Front
Belly
1 piece
Fold
Position

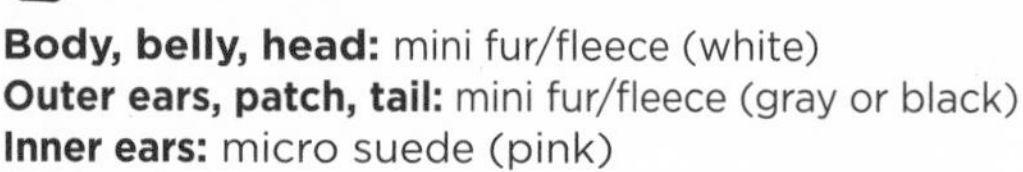

Materials

Body, belly, head: mini fur/fleece (white)
Outer ears, patch, tail: mini fur/fleece (gray or black)
Inner ears: micro suede (pink)
Eyes: onyx beads (1.5 mm)

Finishing

I recommend coloring the tip of the snout and the feet lightly with blush.

Pointers

Patch: Refer to Instruction Pointer 4
Tail: Stuff the tail.

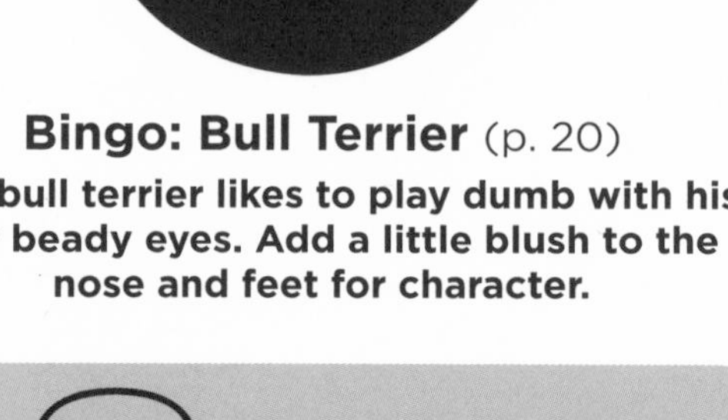
CUTE DOGS
Bingo

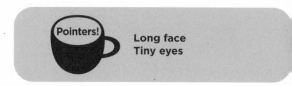

Bingo: Bull Terrier (p. 20)

This bull terrier likes to play dumb with his tiny beady eyes. Add a little blush to the nose and feet for character.

Pointers!
Long face
Tiny eyes

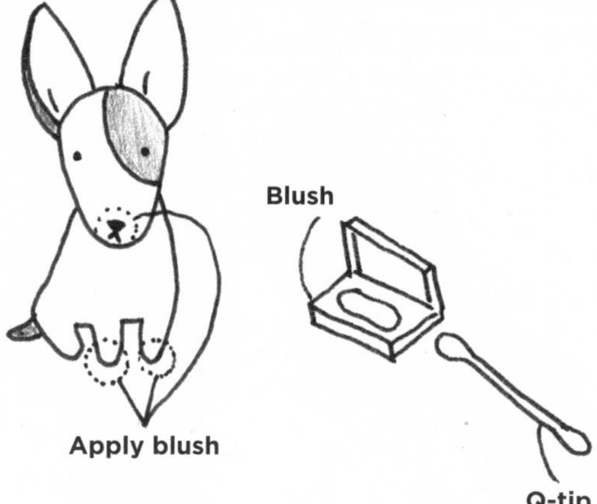
Blush
Apply blush
Q-tip

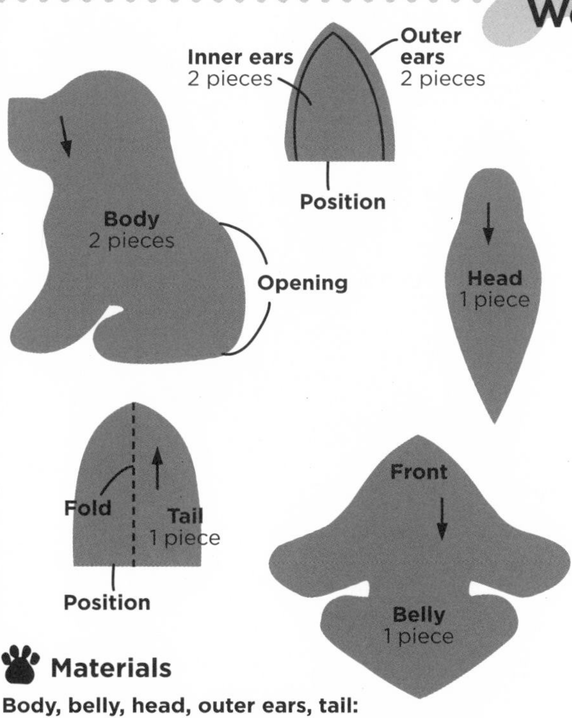
Inner ears
2 pieces
Outer
ears
2 pieces
Position
Body
2 pieces
Opening
Head
1 piece
Fold
Tail
1 piece
Position
Front
Belly
1 piece

Materials

Body, belly, head, outer ears, tail: faux (viscose) fur (white)
Inner ears: ultra suede (pink)
Eyes: onyx beads (1.5 mm)

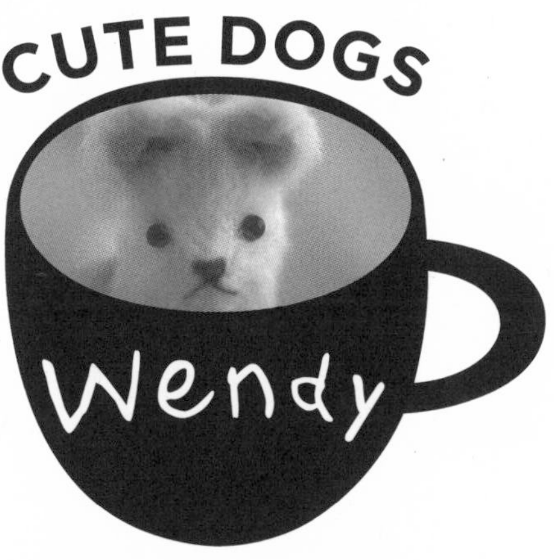
CUTE DOGS
Wendy

Wendy: White Terrier (p. 22)

**I wanted to make an all-white pup.
Brush the tip of the snout.**

Pointer!

Brush the fur at the tip of the snout to direct the fur

Pointer

Treatment of raw edges of faux fur:
Refer to Instruction Pointer 2

Point close-up

Instructions Champ

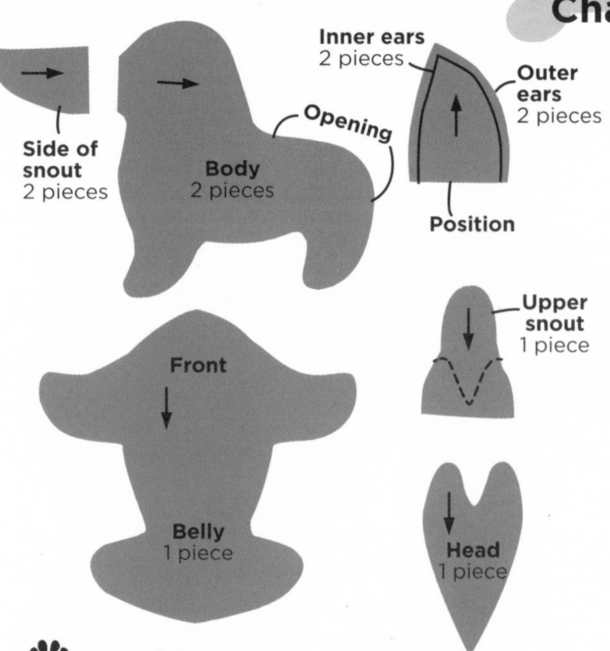

Side of snout
2 pieces
Body
2 pieces
Opening
Inner ears
2 pieces
Outer ears
2 pieces
Position
Front
Belly
1 piece
Upper snout
1 piece
Head
1 piece

CUTE DOGS
Champ

Champ: Welsh Corgi (p. 24)

Corgis' unbalanced physique is so cute it makes me smile. Oh, his legs are so short, and he has no tail. His rear is too cute!

Pointers!

Short legs, large ears, white snout, and no tail.

Materials

Body, head, outer ears: mini fur/fleece (shiny light brown)
Belly, side of the snout, upper snout: mini fur (shiny white)
Inner ears: ultra suede (light pink)
Eyes: onyx beads

Two-color snout

Refer to page 73.
Sew together the sides of the snout and the belly with the fabric reverse-side out.

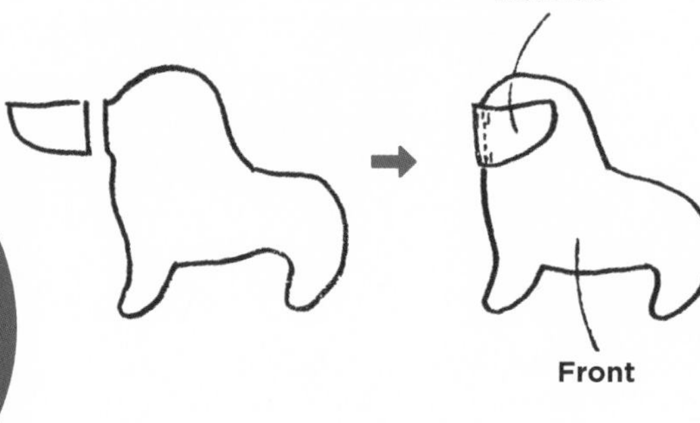

Reverse
Front

Point close-up

Instructions
Pepsi & Coke

Both Pepsi and Coke

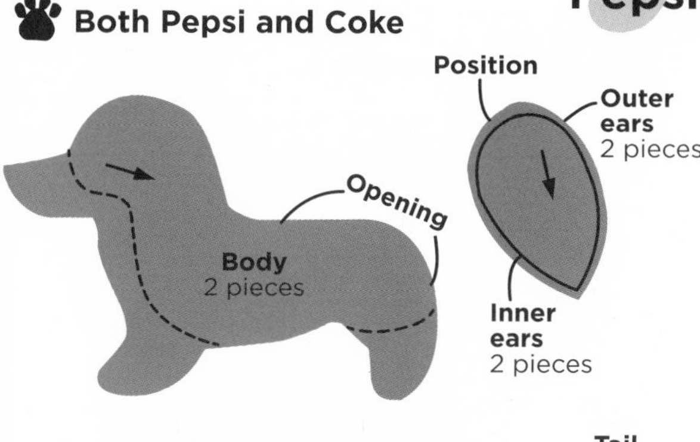
Position
Outer ears
2 pieces
Opening
Body
2 pieces
Inner ears
2 pieces

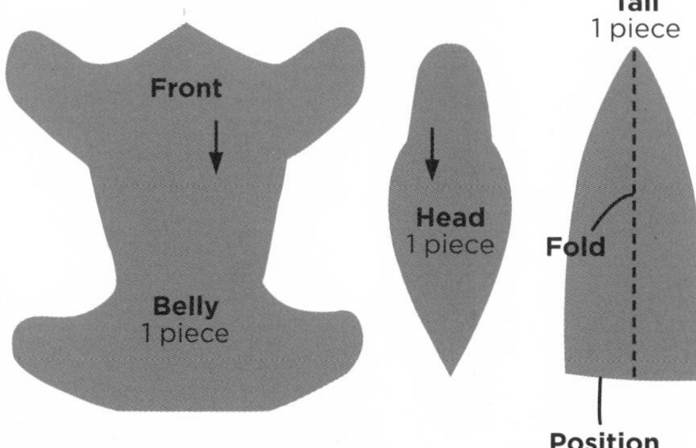
Tail
1 piece
Front
Head
1 piece
Fold
Belly
1 piece
Position

For Coke

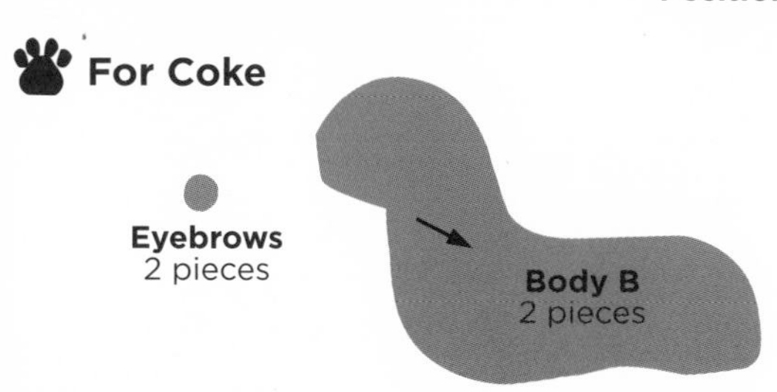
Eyebrows
2 pieces
Body B
2 pieces

Materials

Pepsi
Body, belly, head, outer ears, tail: mini fur/fleece (shiny brown)
Inner ears: micro suede (smoky pink)
Eyes: onyx beads

Coke
Body, belly: mini fur/fleece (shiny brown)
Body B, head, outer ears, tail: mini fur/fleece (shiny black)
Inner ears: micro suede (smoky pink)
Eyebrow spots: micro suede (beige)
Eyes: onyx beads

CUTE DOGS

pepsi & Coke

Pepsi & Coke: Miniature Dachshunds (p. 26)

I see this breed often these days. When I see them running with those short legs as if their lives depended on it, I think to myself, "They're so gallant."

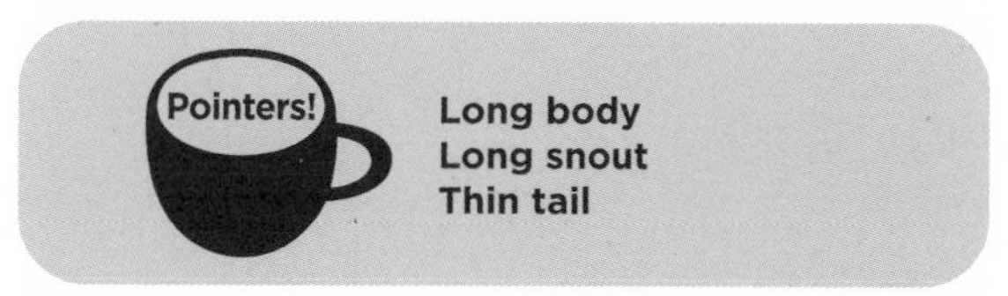
Pointers!
Long body
Long snout
Thin tail

Coke's patches

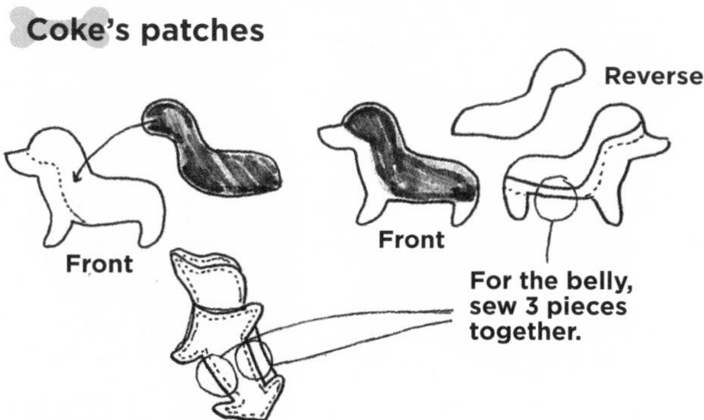
Reverse
Front
Front
For the belly, sew 3 pieces together.

Pointers

How to add eyebrow dots: refer to page 63
Don't stuff the tail.

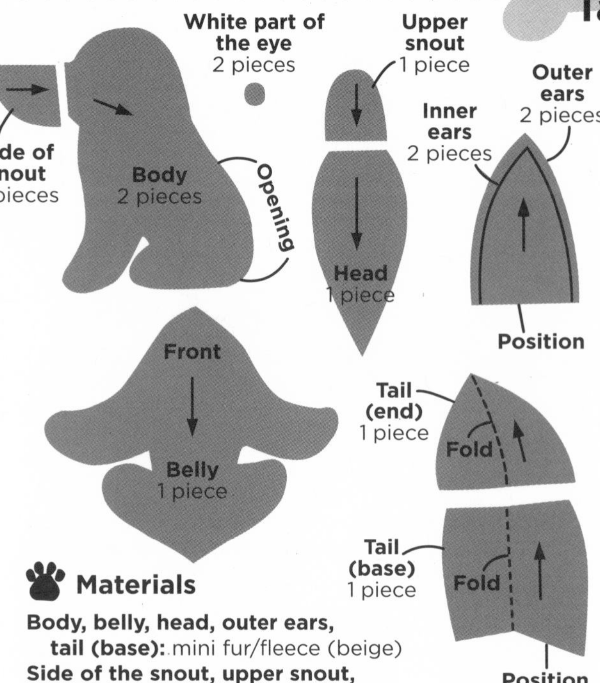

Instructions
Taro
White part of the eye
2 pieces
Upper snout
1 piece
Outer ears
2 pieces
Inner ears
2 pieces
Side of snout
2 pieces
Body
2 pieces
Opening
Head
1 piece
Position
Front
Belly
1 piece
Tail (end)
1 piece
Fold
Tail (base)
1 piece
Fold
Position

CUTE DOGS
Taro

Taro: Mixed breed (p. 28)

Taro is a mixed bred.
I wanted to make a puppy that I would find anywhere with eyebrows, a white snout, and with the name Taro.

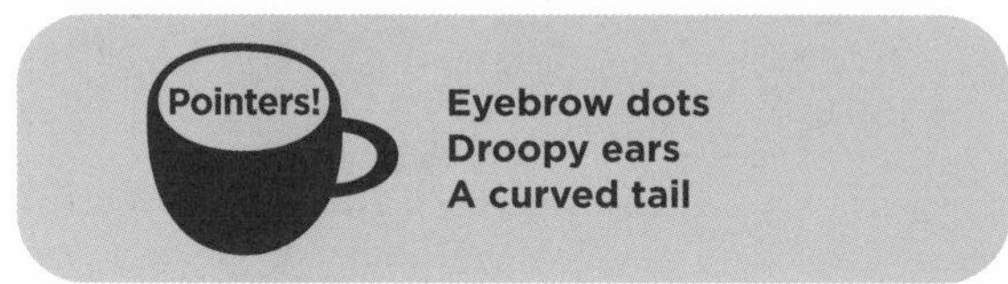

Pointers!
Eyebrow dots
Droopy ears
A curved tail

Materials

Body, belly, head, outer ears, tail (base): mini fur/fleece (beige)
Side of the snout, upper snout, tail (end): mini fur/fleece (white)
Eyebrow dots: micro suede (white)
Inner ears: micro suede (beige)
Eyes: onyx beads

Two-color snout

Refer to page 73.
With the reverse sides out, sew the side of the snout and the body pieces together, and the upper snout and the head pieces together.

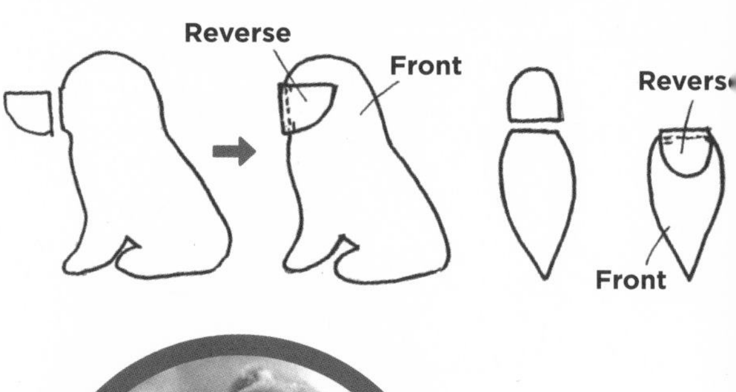

Reverse
Front
Revers
Front

Pointers

Droopy ears: Refer to Instruction Pointer 5
Stuff the tail: Refer to Instruction Pointer 6

Point close-up

Instructions
Robin

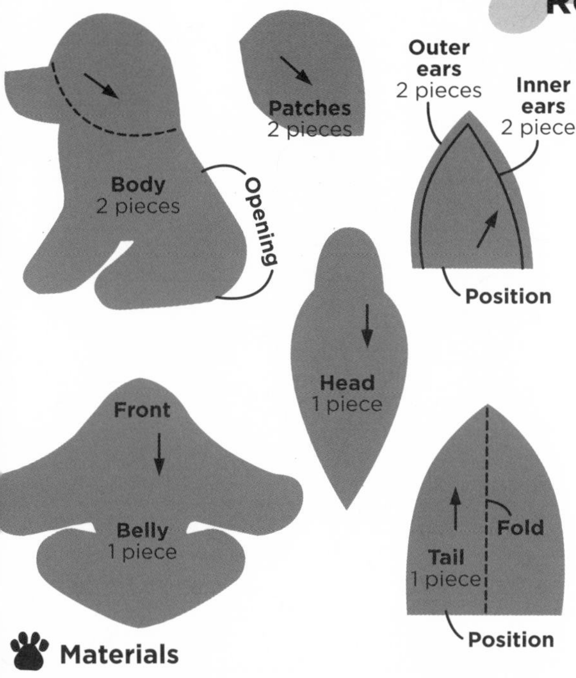

Body
2 pieces
Opening
Patches
2 pieces
Outer ears
2 pieces
Inner ears
2 pieces
Position
Head
1 piece
Front
Belly
1 piece
Tail
1 piece
Fold
Position

Materials

Body, belly, head: faux (viscose) fur (white)
Patches, outer ears, tail: faux (viscose) fur (brown)
Inner ears: ultra suede (pink)
Eyes: onyx beads

CUTE DOGS

Robin

Robin: Papillon (p. 30)

Papillons are lovely with their large ears. These pups are very delicate and I always want to protect them.

Pointers!

Large ears.
Be aware of the hair direction on the ears.

Pointers

Patches: Refer to Instruction Pointer 4
Treatment of raw edges of faux fur:
Refer to Instruction Pointer 2

Point close-up

Instructions
The Three Brothers

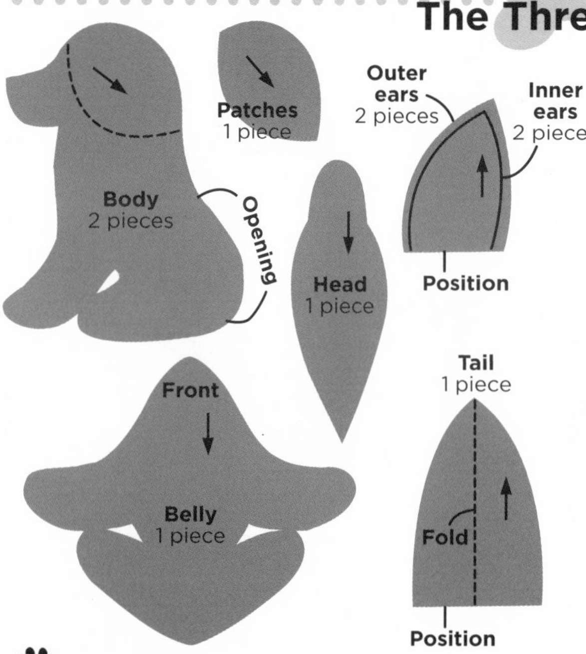

Patches
1 piece
Outer ears
2 pieces
Inner ears
2 pieces
Body
2 pieces
Opening
Head
1 piece
Position
Tail
1 piece
Front
Belly
1 piece
Fold
Position

 **Materials**

Body, belly, head: mini fur/fleece (white)
Patch, outer ears, tail: mini fur/fleece (brown)
Inner ears: ultra suede (pink)
Eyes: onyx beads

Pointers

The patch on the pattern is for Terry.
Patches: Refer to Instruction Pointer 4
Droopy ears: Refer to Instruction Pointer 5
Stuff the tail.

CUTE DOGS
Jack
Terry
Russell

Jack, Terry, and Russell: Jack Russell Terriers (p. 32)

I made them thinking that it would be fun to have the same breed of dogs with slightly different patches sitting next to each other.

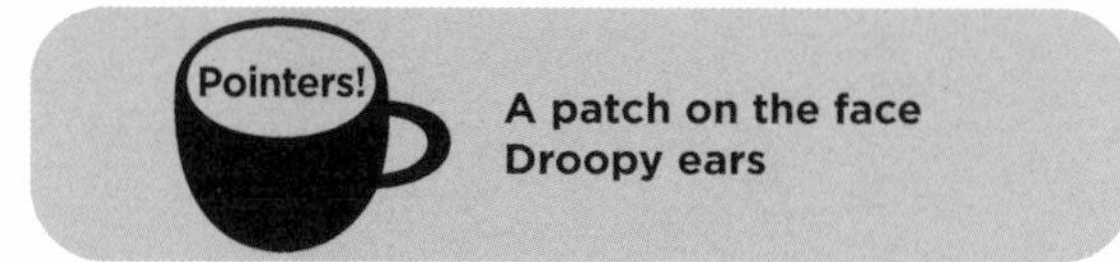

Pointers!
A patch on the face
Droopy ears

Instructions AI

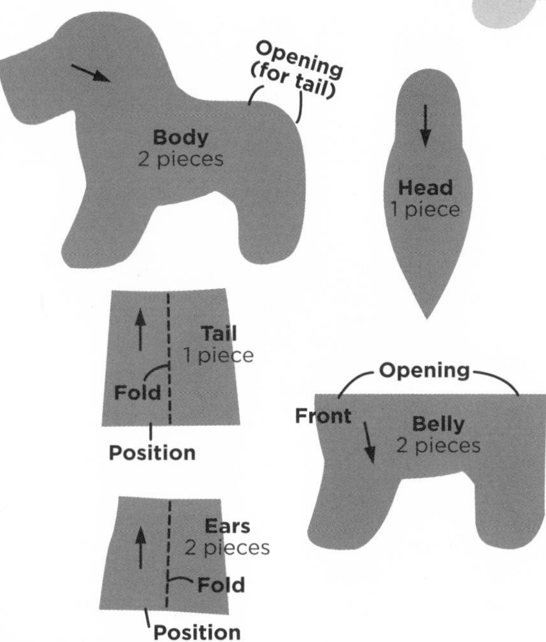

Opening (for tail)
Body
2 pieces
Head
1 piece
Tail
1 piece
Fold
Position
Opening
Front
Belly
2 pieces
Ears
2 pieces
Fold
Position

CUTE DOGS
AI

AI: Wirehaired Fox Terrier (p. 34)

He's spiffy-looking, like he came straight out of a cool movie. He looks so smart dressed up, too.

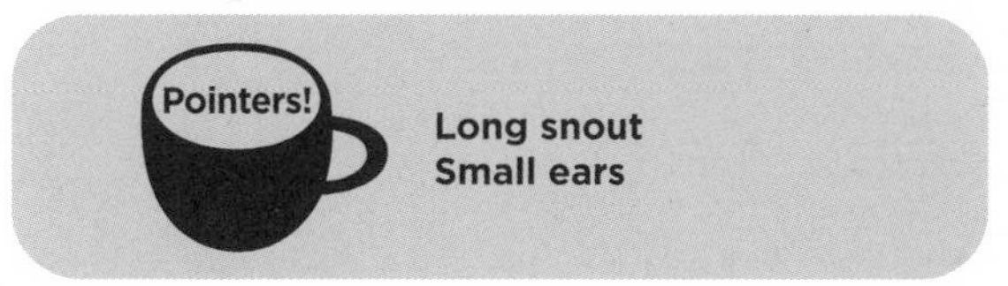

Pointers!
Long snout
Small ears

Materials

Body, belly, head: faux (viscose) fur (white)
Ears, tail: mini fur/fleece (light brown)
Eyes: onyx beads

Ears and the tail

Since it is going to be hard to turn out the fabric for the little ears and the narrow tail, sew them by folding in the seam margins from the front side of the fabric.
Use cross-stitches.

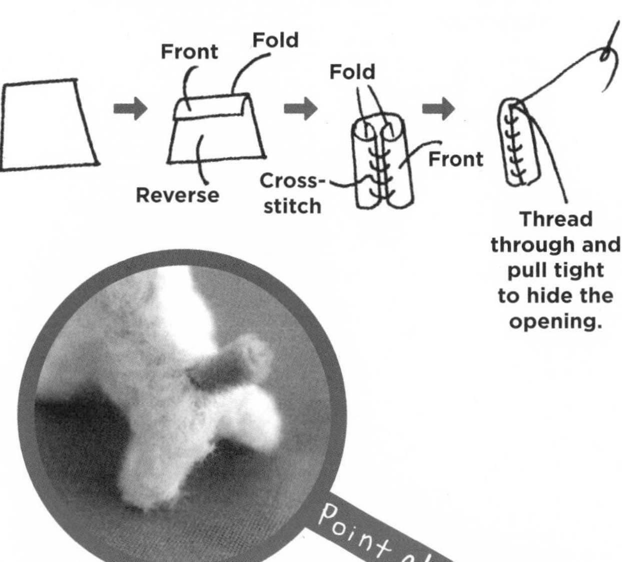

Front
Fold
Fold
Front
Reverse
Cross-stitch
Thread through and pull tight to hide the opening.
Point close-up

Finishing

With faux fur the pile tend to get stuck in the seam, so scoop out the fur that got stuck with a marking pin, etc. at the finishing stage. Afterwards, brush it with a toothbrush.

Pointers

Treatment of the raw edges of faux fur:
Refer to Instruction Pointer 2
Standing pose: Refer to page 77

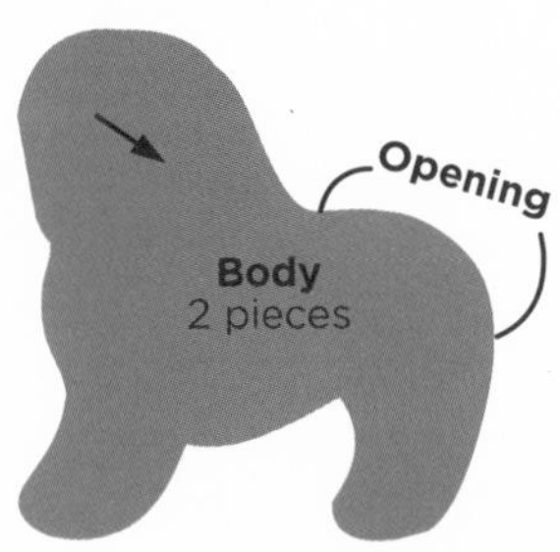
Side of snout
2 pieces
Opening
Body
2 pieces

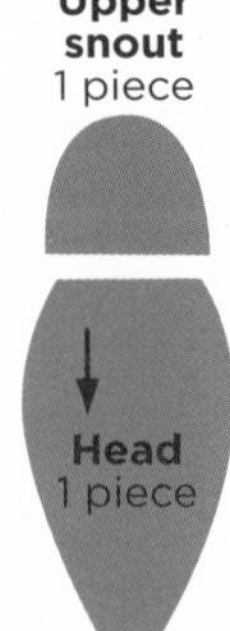
Upper snout
1 piece
Head
1 piece

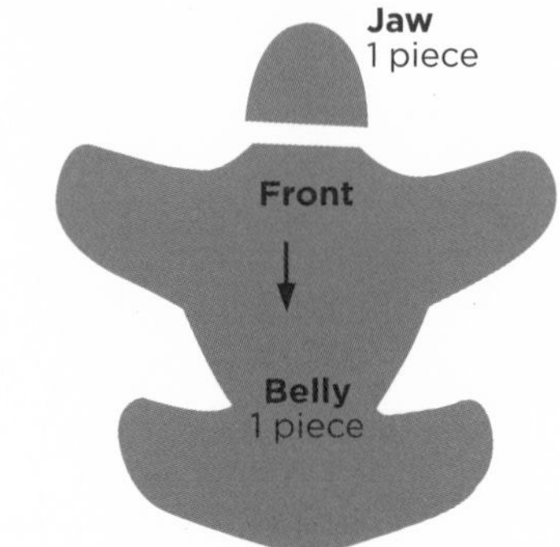
Jaw
1 piece
Front
Belly
1 piece

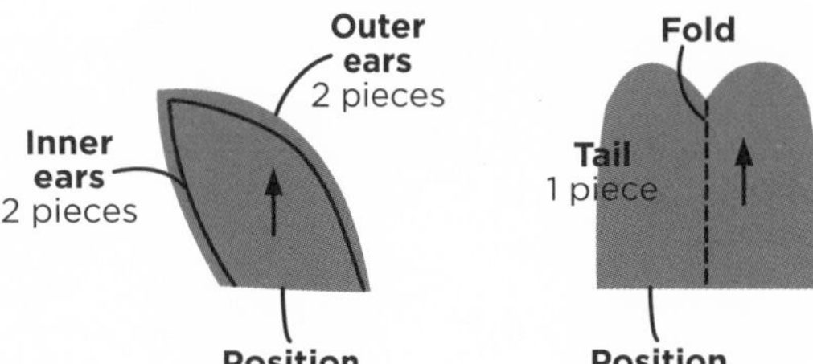
Outer ears
2 pieces
Inner ears
2 pieces
Position
Fold
Tail
1 piece
Position

Materials

Body, belly, head, outer ears: mini fur/fleece (cream)
Side of snout, upper snout, jaw: micro suede (black)
Inner ears: micro suede (smoky pink)
Tail: mini fur/fleece (black)
Eyes: onyx beads

CUTE DOGS
puddin

Puddin: Pug (p. 36)

What's charming about pugs is that they have a plump body and strong shoulders—and a perpetual look of worry. They're so cute. I like teasing them.

Pointers!

Googly-eyed
Strong shoulders
Short tail
Squished-in snout

Pug's snout

❶ With the reverse side out, sew the body and the sides of the snout together, the belly and the jaw together, and the head and the upper snout together.

❷ With the reverse sides of the jaw and the left side of the snout out, sew from the edge of the belly to point A, which is at the center of the jaw. Next, sew the right side of the snout up to point A.

❸ With the reverse sides of the right and the left side of the snout facing out, sew the remaining length from point A to point B.

❹ With the reverse sides of the upper snout and the sides of the snout facing out, sew the right and left sides of the body to the head, starting from point B on the side of the snout. Refer to pages 55 and 56 for sewing techniques.

❺ After stuffing, insert the needle from the back of the head and pull out from the top of the snout. Then, insert the needle again on the other side of the top of the snout out back through to the back of the head. Pull the thread tight—this will give the snout wrinkles and turn it upward, making it look like a pug.

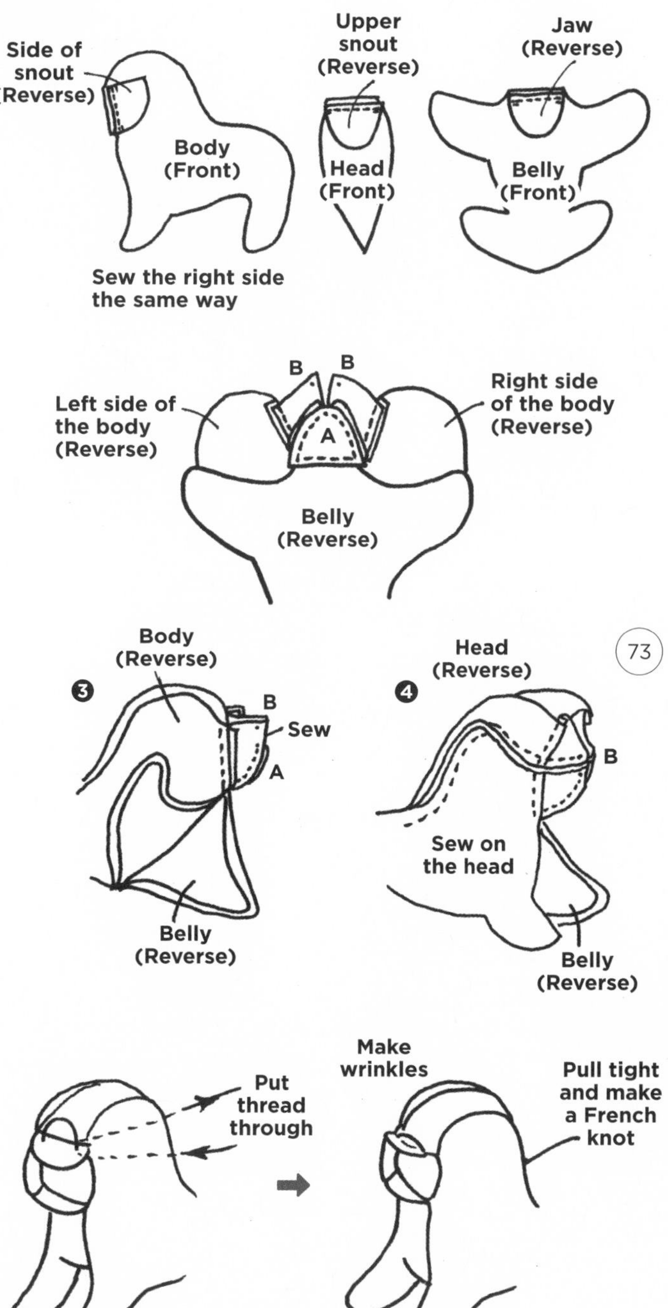
Side of snout (Reverse)
Upper snout (Reverse)
Jaw (Reverse)
Body (Front)
Head (Front)
Belly (Front)
Sew the right side the same way
B
B
Left side of the body (Reverse)
A
Right side of the body (Reverse)
Belly (Reverse)
Body (Reverse)
❸
B
Sew
A
Belly (Reverse)
Head (Reverse)
❹
B
Sew on the head
Belly (Reverse)
Put thread through
Make wrinkles
Pull tight and make a French knot

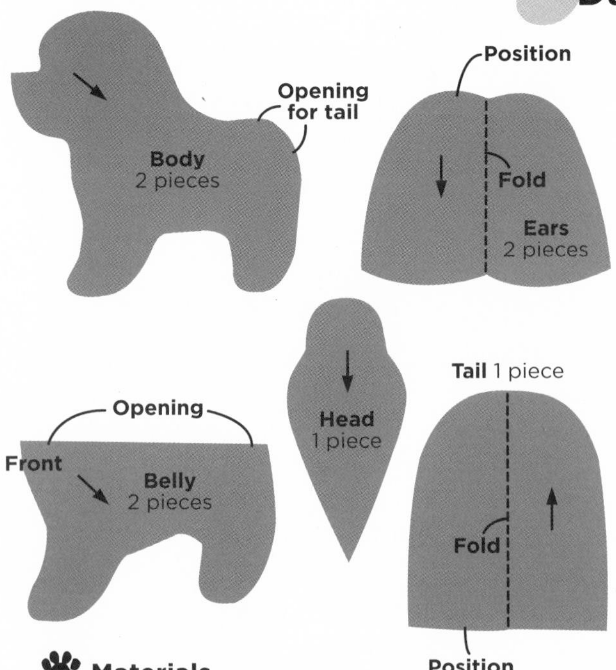
Body
2 pieces
Opening
for tail
Position
Fold
Ears
2 pieces
Head
1 piece
Tail 1 piece
Opening
Front
Belly
2 pieces
Fold
Position

Materials

Body, belly, head: faux (viscose) fur (white)
Ears, tail: faux (viscose) fur (cocoa)
Eyes: onyx beads

How to attach the eyes

It's cute if you attach the eyes just above the nose.

Pointers

Treatment of the raw edges of faux fur:
Refer to Instruction Pointer 2
Standing pose: Refer to page 77
Curled tail: Refer to page 61

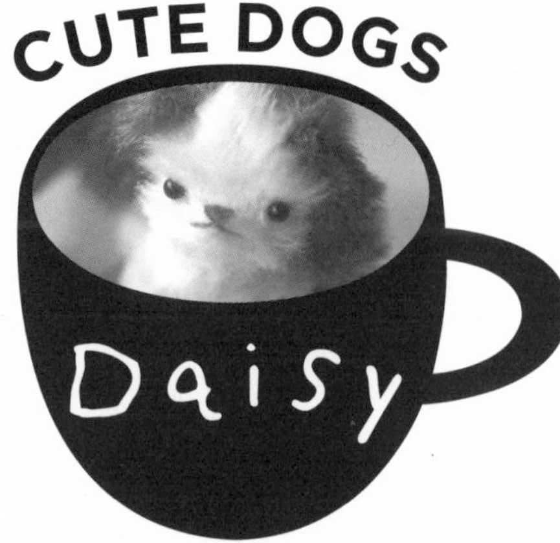
CUTE DOGS
Daisy

Daisy: Shih Tzu (p. 38)

What's cute about Shih Tzus is that they give an impression that they're strong-minded and sassy.

Pointers!
Squished-in snout
A curled tail

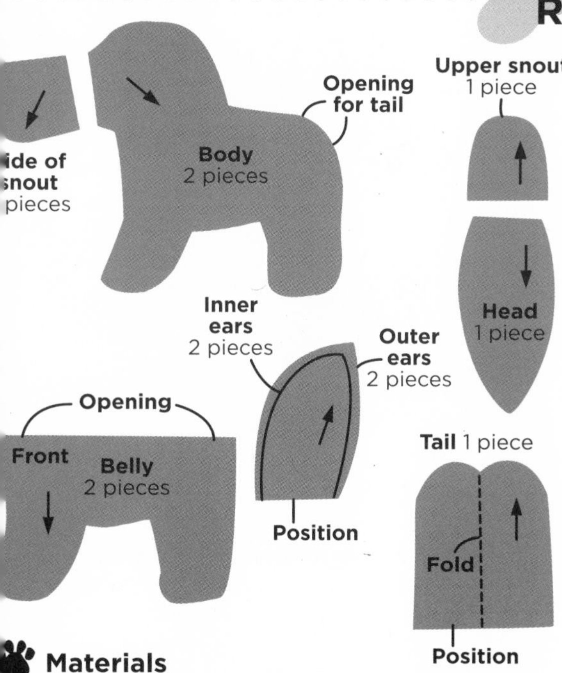
Side of snout
2 pieces
Body
2 pieces
Opening for tail
Upper snout
1 piece
Head
1 piece
Inner ears
2 pieces
Outer ears
2 pieces
Opening
Front
Belly
2 pieces
Position
Tail 1 piece
Fold
Position

CUTE DOGS
Raoul

Raoul: Miniature Schnauzer (p. 40)

Schnauzers have a philosophical air. Perhaps they're really happy-go-lucky and just seem like deep-thinkers.

Pointer!
The pile direction at the snout

Materials

Body, belly, head, outer ears, tail: faux (viscose) fur (gray)
Side of the snout, upper snout: faux (viscose) fur (white)
Inner ears: micro suede (smoky pink)
Eyes: onyx beads

Direction of fur

The schnauzer's beard-like fur can be achieved by reversing the pile direction on the head and the snout. Take note of the pile direction when cutting the fabric. For eyebrows, at the finishing stage, pinch the pile above the eyes with your thumb and forefinger to make it go against the pile direction. Here, since I couldn't find a piece of fabric in just the right color, I colored a piece of white fur by soaking it a few times in ink.

Pointers

Treatment of the raw edges of viscose fabric:
Refer to Instruction Pointer 2
Droopy ears: Refer to Instruction Pointer 5
Standing pose: Refer to page 77

Pinch it with your thumb and forefinger to make it go against the pile direction.
When cutting the fabric, be aware of the pile direction.

Instructions
Puppies

CUTE DOGS
CUTE DOGS
CUTE DOGS
puppies

Puppies (p. 43)
Since they're puppies, they're even smaller.

For standing and lying poses

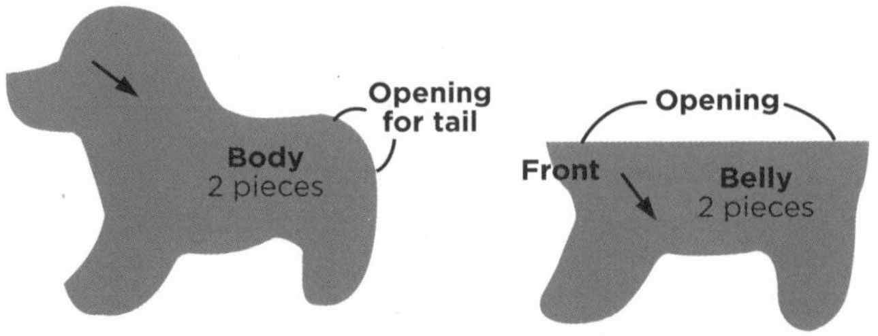

Opening for tail
Body 2 pieces

Opening
Front
Belly 2 pieces

For sitting pose

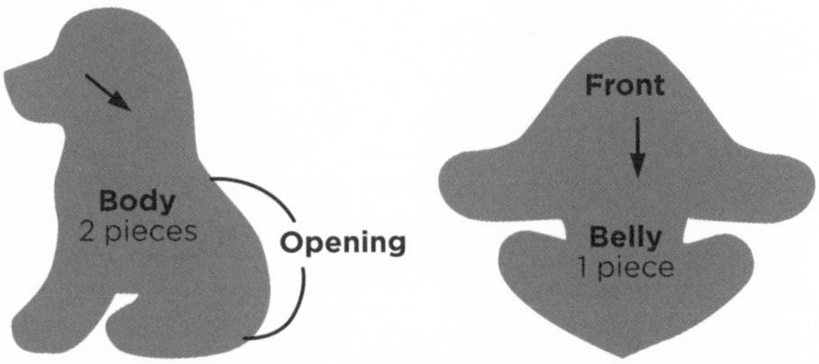

Body 2 pieces
Opening

Front
Belly 1 piece

For all

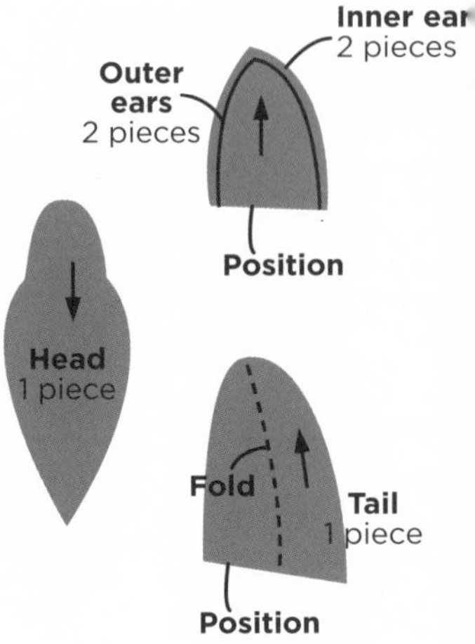

Inner ear 2 pieces
Outer ears 2 pieces
Position

Head 1 piece

Fold
Tail 1 piece
Position

Instructions
Puppies

Materials

Standing Pose
Body, head, outer ears, tail: mini fur/fleece (cocoa)
Belly: mini fur/fleece (white)
Inner ears: micro suede (smoky pink)
Eyes: onyx beads

Lying Pose
Body, head, outer ears, tail: mini fur/fleece (ochre)
Belly: mini fur/fleece (white)
Inner ears: micro suede (smoky pink)
Eyes: onyx beads

Sitting Pose
Body, belly, head, tail: mini fur/fleece (white)
Outer ears: mini fur/fleece (cocoa)
Inner ears: ultra suede (smoky pink)
Eyes: onyx beads

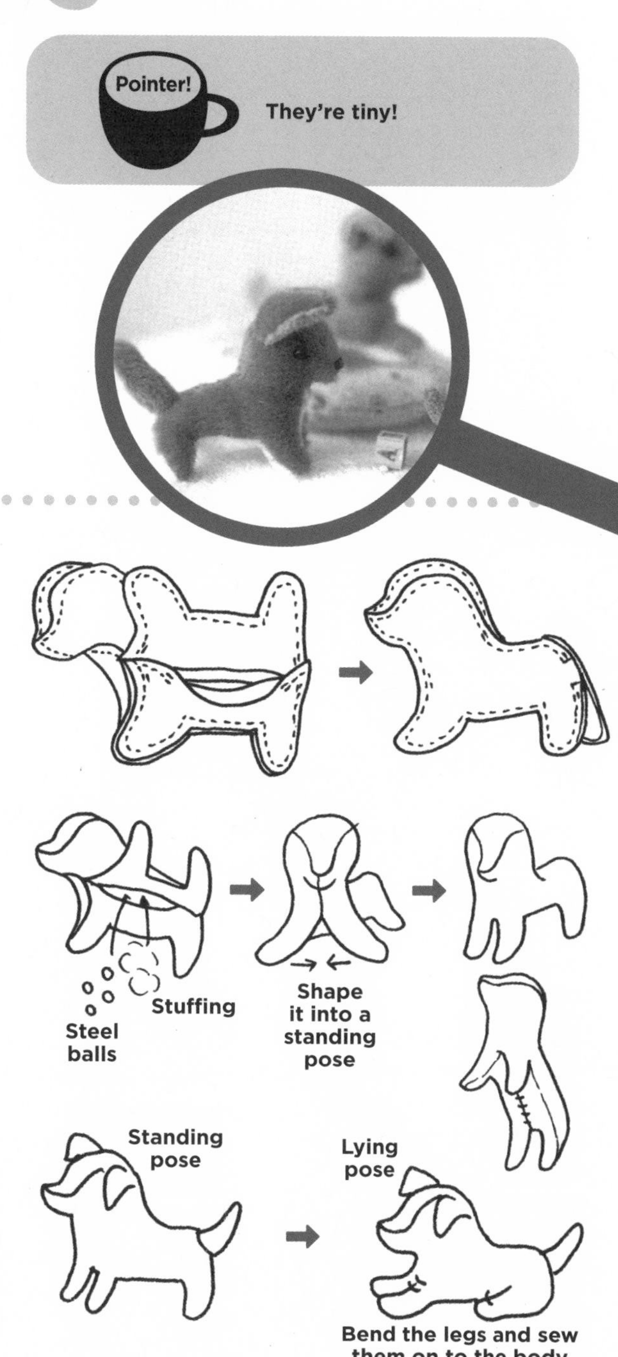

Pointer!
They're tiny!
Stuffing
Steel balls
Shape it into a standing pose
Standing pose
Lying pose
Bend the legs and sew them on to the body

For standing pose and in lying pose

❶ With the reverse sides of the body and the left and right parts of the belly facing out, sew the edges together (except for the opening). This way, it's easier to turn out the fabric since the opening will be large. When dealing with something too small or when the fabric tends to unravel, this method is best.

❷ Next, sew the back closed, except for the tail opening.

❸ After turning it right side out, starting with the tip of the snout and the tip of the legs firmly stuff it with cotton and steel balls through the opening in the belly. Close the opening using ladder stitches.

❹ For the lying pose, insert the needle at the underside where the leg joins the body, bend the legs, and sew the legs onto the body.

Pointers

Droopy ears: Refer to Instruction Pointer 5

Instructions
Ritz and Snow

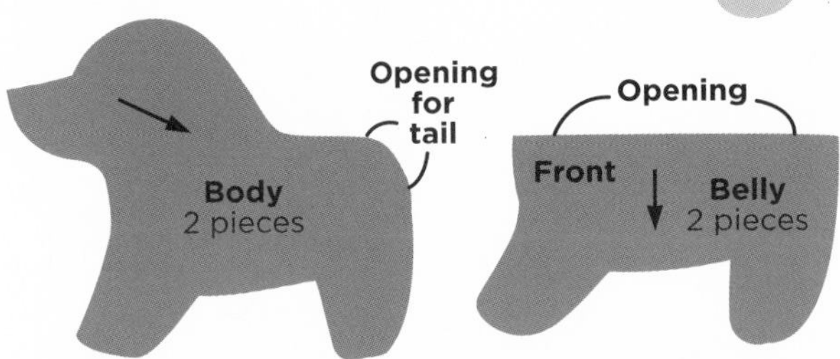

Opening for tail
Opening
Body
2 pieces
Front
Belly
2 pieces

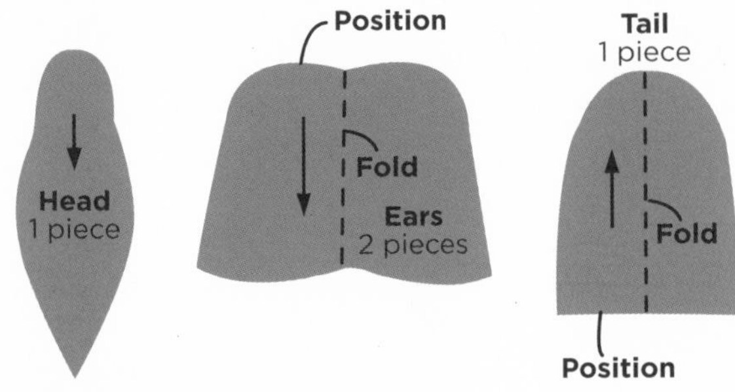

Position
Tail
1 piece
Head
1 piece
Fold
Ears
2 pieces
Fold
Position

Materials

Body, belly, head, ears, tail:
faux (viscose) fur (brown for Ritz, white for Snow)
Eyes: glass eyes

CUTE DOGS
Ritz &
Snow

Ritz and Snow (p. 42)

In faux fur with glass eyes, they have a European air to them.

Pointers!

Tiny bodies
Large eyes
Droopy ears
A ribbon

How to attach glass eyes

Cut the wire about 2/5" (1 cm) carefully so as not to break the glass, and make a loop using pliers. Poke a hole with an awl where you want the eyes, insert the glass eyes, and pull the thread towards the back of the head to attach.

Pointers

They're similar to the puppies, but they turned out to look like indoor dogs when I used a different material to make the droopy ears. You can make them even cuter by adding a ribbon.

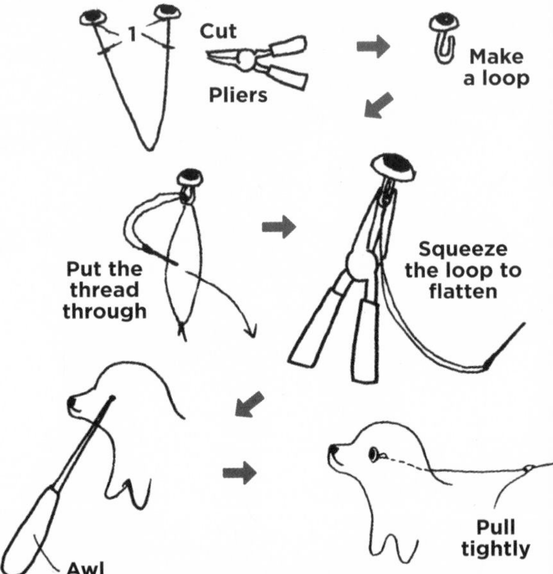

1
Cut
Pliers
Make a loop
Put the thread through
Squeeze the loop to flatten
Awl
Pull tightly

Chie Hayano

Born in 1971. She loves handcrafting, drawing pictures, and small things. She started making miniature stuffed animals in 1998. Participated in miniature craft competitions under the name "Soramame Studio." She has also presented her work on her official website. Her aim is to create works with presence which, even if they're small, expand people's imaginations.

Soramame Studio
http://www01.u-page.so-net.ne.jp/zd5/soramame/

Afterword...

"Would you like to write a book about miniature stuffed animals?" read the email that I received from the publisher one night. I couldn't believe that such a thing—like hitting the jackpot—could happen to me! On top of that, they were asking me to make a craft book! Even better! Wow! I hadn't used patterns for my crafted animals. I just put scissors to fabric straightaway when I came up with an idea, followed my instincts in sewing them, and ended up with the chance to write this book. There were many times when I was on the verge of tears and thought to myself that the scale of this was beyond me. The reason I was able to somehow put my ideas into shape was that I had various people's support and backup and guidance. To friends and family members who always cheered me on, I would like to say, "Thank you so much."

CUTE
DOGS

Cute Dogs
Craft Your Own Pooches

Translation: Molly Kiser

Published by Vertical, Inc., New York.

Originally published in Japanese as
Nuigurumino Chiisana Chiisana Wanko Tachi, Mamegurumi
by Bunka Shuppankyoku, Tokyo, 2001.

ISBN 978-1-934287-67-5

Manufactured in The United States of America

First American Edition

Vertical, Inc.
www.vertical-inc.com